D1500374

SHOWING *for* BEGINNERS

HALLIE I. McEvoy

The Lyons Press

DEDICATION

To my parents, Paula and Gunther Hertwig, who let me keep a horse in the backyard while growing up. They have now realized the "horse phase" of my adolescence is unending; and to my beloved husband, Thom, who puts up with my "horse habit" and is kind enough not to notice the hay and shavings on the floor in the living room.

Printed in the United States of America
Illustrations © by Laurie Harden
Design by Elaine Streithof

10 9 8 7 6 5 4 3

Library of Congress Cataloging-in-Publication Data

McEvoy, Hallie I.
    Showing for beginners / Hallie I. McEvoy.
        p.   cm.
    Includes index.
    ISBN 1-55821-500-X (pb)
    1. Horses—Showing. 2. Show riding. I. Title.
SF295.M34 1996
798.2'4—dc20   96-30498
                                                                        CIP

Hailey

CONTENTS

ACKNOWLEDGMENTS

A BOOK DOES NOT GET WRITTEN without the inspiration of many people. I wish to thank:

Fellow judges and stewards Victor Hugo-Vidal, Rita Timpanaro, Pattie Auricchio, Jackie Martin, Kathy Kennett, Beth I. Stoltz, Don Tobey, Ellie Estes, Diane Guiliano Cockburn, and Connie Lacy Herrick, for freely sharing their knowledge and expertise;

Riding instructors and coaches Sheila Rodgers of Good Shepherd Farm, Suzanne Reilly of Fred's Farm, Joan Starck of Navajo Farm, Kimberly Irish of Kimberly Irish Show Stables, Pattie and Joe Forest of Horton Farm, Laura Reimer of Victory Farms, Beth Phalen of Mad River Stables, and the late Robert Hoskins, for their teaching methods and friendship;

Secretary to the AHSA Licensed Officials Committee Marilynn Glick, for her unfailing good humor and graciousness in answering my constant queries;

USET Public Relations Director Marty Bauman and author Steven D. Price, for their encouragement;

Dawn Laliberte, editor of *The Morgan Horse*, and John Raaf, publisher of *HorsePlay*, for giving me space to write in their wonderful publications;

The editor of this book, Lilly Golden, for her incredible patience with a first-time author;

Family and friends Hope Barry, Heidi Hertwig, Hilde Arnao, Inge and Werner Hotrich, Elaine Pollak, Liz Miller, Judith Wyman Strobridge, Beverly McMullin, the Peplowskis, Sewards, Littles, Amarantes-McCormacks, and Grahams, for always believing in me and giving me constant support—in the saddle and out;

And finally, five of the finest horsemen in the world, Floyd Fuller, Ted Landers, Ellen P. Keith, and Bernie and Trudy Cohen, for giving me an ideal to strive for.

FOREWORD

WHAT AN ABSOLUTE DELIGHT it is to read Hallie McEvoy's Showing for Beginners. Had there only been a book of this type when I was turning thirteen and beginning to show, I would have been saved much trial and error and put in a more positive frame of mind. Since there were not any how-to-show books available, I simply had to wing it and hope for the best. For every few steps of progress forward, there was all too often a step back due to ignorance.

Two suggestions in the book that I feel are especially important are, first, to enjoy oneself and be happy, and, second, to breathe. At this later stage of my life, these seem so simple to me, but unfortunately when I was a teenager and a competitor neither of these precepts ever crossed my mind. Consequently I was always extremely solemn and brusque to my parents—I felt they were absolutely ignorant when it came to anything equine. In all fairness to them, horseback riding was not their specialty, and although they permitted me to ride and take lessons, they really considered it a phase I would outgrow. (Little did they know! Having turned my avocation into my profession, I'm having more fun than any adult should be allowed.) Had this book been available to my parents, we could have enjoyed horse showing as a family sport. It would have furnished the knowledge and experience that they lacked, and for which I, as a spoiled only child, never forgave them.

As for breathing, I used to think that being short-winded was a natural occurrence. I would practice holding my breath by swimming underwater for longer and longer periods, thinking that I had to increase my lung capacity so I wouldn't turn beet red and almost pass out before my jumping course was finished. Obviously, innocence is not always bliss. Now, in both my teaching and judging, I am aware of people holding their breath, and work hard at getting them to relax and inhale and exhale normally. Adults, especially those taking up riding as a new sport, are prone to this kind of tension, and must be taught to loosen up. I suggest that they talk while they ride, since it is impossible to hold one's breath while conversing. Had I but known about breathing in my youth, how much simpler my competitive riding life would have been.

Another valuable feature of this book is the chapter on buying the right horse, the responsibilities of the trainer and the veterinarian in the transaction, and all the particulars involved. Had my parents read Hallie's book first, it would have precluded their purchase of the very beautiful but lame gelding that was my surprise nineteenth-birthday present. It's very hard to get rid of a chronically lame horse (even if he is very handsome) once the dealer who unscrupulously sells it to nice but unknowing parents says it isn't his responsibility anymore . . .

I had forgotten that the myriad unrelated things having to do with horse shows—which become second nature after a while—can be overwhelming to a novice. The many strange words and phrases that comprise the showing vernacular, the correct attire, filling out entry blanks (not my favorite chore)—these and all the various things in between are covered with humor and in detail in the following pages.

Having judged with Hallie, I know of her sincerity and enjoyment of the sport, and of her delicious sense of humor. These all come across loud and clear in her book. Hallie wisely conveys the importance of being able to chuckle at a mistake of one's own doing—or of someone else's, for that matter. Realizing that an error is not the end of the world certainly puts things in their proper perspective.

All in all, this book is a must for anyone recently introduced to showing, whether young or old. It also should be read in its entirety by the people closest to these newcomers, including but not limited to parents, spouses, siblings, and children. It should also be read by trainers and coaches. It is enlightening to walk a mile in someone else's riding boots, as it is easy to forget how things that have become ingrained habits for some can be a complete puzzle to the uninitiated.

Victor Hugo-Vidal
Dana Point, California
Fall 1996

INTRODUCTION

SHOWING SHOULD BE FUN. Sometimes this simple fact gets lost in the hustle and bustle. Why would anyone in his or her right mind get up so early in the morning (on a weekend!) and go through such aggravation to show a horse? It must be fun.

This book is not designed to teach you to ride, or to give you the fine points of subtle aids, leg placement, and indirect reining. There are many fine books available for all that. (Three of the best are Waldemar Seunig's *Horsemanship,* Nuno Oliveria's *Reflections on Equestrian Art,* and George Morris's *Hunter Seat Equitation.*) Nor will this be an in-depth examination of showing at the upper levels, with photographs of experts jumping 5-foot fences. There are plenty of books on that topic as well.

The purpose here is to introduce, motivate, and prepare beginners of any age for the elegant, mysterious, and wonderful world of horse showing. The principle that guides this book is that horse showing should be fun and accessible for everyone.

Horse showing is a sport that attracts people of all ages. Whether you're six or sixty, there's a horse show division that will fit your budget, ability, and interest. Many people think that they'll try showing once, just to see what it's all about. But horse shows are like potato chips—you can't stop at one.

The fastest growing segment of the riding population is beginner adult riders. Very often, they are the parents of children who are riding and showing. Horse shows are more enjoyable when everyone in the family takes part. Many shows now have divisions strictly for beginner adults, with whimsical names like the "long stirrup division" (as opposed to "short stirrup," which is for children).

Many adult beginners have had no previous connection to horses at all. Perhaps they wanted ponies when they were children, or have always liked animals. No matter why or how they start riding and showing, adults find out quickly what has attracted countless scores of children to the sport. It provides good exercise, a healthy competitive outlet, a social atmosphere, and a wonderful opportunity to enjoy teamwork and the companionship of your horse.

Children and horses are still the main focus of most shows. Kids as young as two years old can be seen on their adorable ponies in the lead line division. Six-year-olds can often be seen jumping their ponies over courses of fences in the pony hunter division. Then there are the elegant, teenage equitation riders. They ride their steeds over fences of 3'6" and compete against the best riders in the nation in the American Horse Shows Association (AHSA) Medal and American Society for the Prevention of Cruelty to Animals (ASPCA) Maclay classes.

Even if a child doesn't continue riding and showing, lessons learned will resonate for years to come. The traits of good sportsmanship, teamwork, flexibility, and the ability to work hard can all be learned at a horse show. Most important, the memories of the fun and accomplishments will stay with a child forever.

No matter how you or your children perform at a show, remember to keep that little word, *fun,* in the picture. Many events in life deserve to be taken seriously, but certainly not horse shows. Keep your goals at the show in perspective and have a good time.

I love the sport of showing horses from all perspectives—as judge, competitor, and spectator. I'm grateful to all my instructors and coaches, but especially to the ones who taught me as a beginner to love showing. Nancy Peters of Ketchum Pony Farm in Fort Salonga, New York, took me to my first horse show. I will never forget how excited I was or the good time I had. I rode a big, chestnut horse named Cavalier who I thought was the greatest horse in the world. (Of course, once I got my own horse, Dr. Doolittle, *he* became the best horse in the world.)

That show was held at another small, local stable, Little Plains Stable in Greenlawn, New York. Run by Joan Krogmann for over thirty years, Little Plains started many riders on successful show careers. Both these wonderful neighborhood stables are long gone, replaced, at least in part, by housing developments. But the love of showing endures for me, as it does for hundreds of others who rode and showed at these and other such stables across the country.

My first real show coach was the exacting and talented Lee Krantz. Lee had a distinguished show career, then turned to teaching. She taught me the value of hard work, discipline, and the joy of a well-ridden course. Even now, whether I'm competing or judging, Miss Lee is in the back of my mind with her humane sensitivity and professionalism.

Perhaps the greatest thrill of my beginner riding and show years was meeting legendary national champions Rodney Jenkins and Idle Dice. The pair were showing in a Grand Prix near my home, and I begged a ride to the show. I'll never forget patting Idle Dice and the kindness of Rodney—I was in heaven.

I hope that you, too, will find teachers, mentors, and horses who inspire you and help you pursue your dreams. Now, get out there and show!

Hallie McEvoy
Fall 1996

CHAPTER ONE

Getting Started

THE URGE TO SHOW A HORSE may come upon you suddenly. You see a film clip of a dashing horse and rider, and think, "I want to do that!" Or the feeling may creep up on you slowly, after months or even years of riding lessons. Regardless of your past experiences, showing horses can be fun, exciting, and habit-forming, or, unfortunately, dull, anxiety-provoking, and even downright unpleasant. The difference lies in the amount of preparation and the mental attitude of the rider.

People who ride only as a means to show generally don't get as much enjoyment out of it as those who show as an extension of their love of riding. Those who truly love to show also love horses and the science of riding. A natural extension of successful riding lessons is to want to display what you and your horse have accomplished. Showing also gives the bonus of an evaluation from an impartial observer, the judge. This feedback can be important in advancing your expertise and enjoyment of the sport. Even if you have a poor outing, there's something positive to be learned at every show.

There are certain essential steps that need to be followed to ensure a happy outcome in the show ring. Taking riding lessons, finding a show coach, having a healthy riding exercise program, and adhering to safety in the saddle will lead to a successful outcome—you having fun with your horse in the show ring.

Catherine B. Knight

A riding lesson.

RIDING LESSONS

The best way to get started is to take lessons. Lessons are especially important in riding, because you're contending not only with your own body movements, but with those of a thousand-pound animal as well. This animal has a mind and agenda of his own and, if not handled properly, can be dangerous. Lessons increase your ability to learn and will help prevent injuries.

Some people scoff that riders are not athletes because they think the horse does all the work, but riding is a rigorous sport. Up to five hundred calories an hour can be burned off posting to the trot. The best riders are also very fit. Most of the members of the United States Equestrian Team (USET) combine weight training and aerobics or running to be as fit as they can for riding. However, riding itself is great exercise. It tones the legs and buttocks, improves cardiovascular fitness, and also enhances balance and eye-hand coordination.

Riding lessons should be both a challenge and a joy. Many people who get on a horse without a starter lesson have an unpleasant experience. How many times have you heard stories about horses brushing riders off on trees, planting all four feet and refusing to move, bucking, or running away with riders? Perhaps you've experienced this yourself. Most of these bad first impressions could have been avoided with just a few lessons. Even if you don't wish to become an expert, a few lessons will help you to be a safe and confident casual rider.

Some of the saddest experiences I'm familiar with involve individuals who purchased a horse without having ridden, let alone had a lesson. These hapless souls discovered that owning and riding a horse are not easy. Several of them sold or gave away their horses, and walked away from horses and riding altogether. But the majority of horse dealers, trainers, and instructors are honorable, and would never sell a horse to someone they know has never ridden. (If you hear of anyone who has a reputation for doing business in this manner, steer clear!)

If you're already in a satisfactory lesson program, skip ahead to the next section. If not, read on for some tips on finding a good lesson stable and instructor.

Where can you find a place to take riding lessons? Even in the heart of big cities there are riding academies. Look in your phone book in the Yellow Pages under "Riding Academies," "Riding," "Horses," or "Stables." Call and ask about rates and special learn-to-ride packages. Some stables offer special women- or men-only groups, for people who are more comfortable with that arrangement. Some have evening ride-and-socialize programs where you bring a potluck dish to share after the lesson. There are even family nights at some barns, designed to get the whole family out and riding together. Many stables

Hallie McEvoy

Riding instructor Lisa Divoll demonstrates correct hand position to eight-year-old Laura Matteri, mounted on Nina, a twenty-five year old half Thoroughbred, half Quarter Horse. Laura has a very good basic position for a beginner.

will sell packages of five or ten lessons at a discounted rate. Inquire if beginners are welcome and what opportunities there are to show and compete at the stable. Not all good stables advertise, so don't avoid a stable just because you haven't seen an advertisement for it.

Another resource for finding a riding academy is word of mouth. Ask friends and family members if they know anyone who rides. A direct recommendation is a good way to find a reliable program that fits your needs and budget. Don't be afraid to ask people who are involved with horses what may sound like silly questions. "Were you scared the first time you got on a horse? How expensive is it? What does falling off feel like? Do you like your instructor?"

Tack shops are another resource for finding a riding program. The employees know all the local stables and instructors, and usually can give solid advice. You can also call the American Riding Instructors Certification Program (see appendix) to learn of instructors in your area.

After you've narrowed the field to two or three choices, go to each stable and watch some lessons. Do the riding instructors treat the horses and students with kindness and respect? Is fun emphasized along with learning? Check the stabling. Even if you've never been inside a stable, you should be able to tell if the place is organized and well managed. Is the barn clean? Are the horses well fed and groomed? Go with your instincts as to what program will work best for you.

Expect to pay from $10 all the way up to $50 an hour for a group lesson. Hour-long private lessons can range from $20 to over $100. Beginner lessons should cost at the low end of the scale. The higher prices are for well-known instructors and show coaching, something you may be interested in later on in your riding adventures.

Basic equipment for lessons includes safety helmets, long pants, and hard-soled shoes with a low heel. As you progress, you'll probably want to invest in breeches (pronounced *britch-es*) and riding boots for added comfort and support. Chaps are also excellent to ride in; they help protect your pants and give additional grip on the saddle. Never ride in shorts; you can develop saddle sores—nasty blisters on the insides of your legs.

Riding lessons should teach you the basics of riding and horse-

Hallie McEvoy

Two young riders Allison Staab and Laura Matteri, appropriately dressed for a beginner lesson. Both are wearing form-fitting pants and shirts, hard soled, ankle-high boots with heels, and riding helmets with safety harnesses. Note that they are both holding the reins correctly and safely.

Hallie McEvoy

Adult rider Karen Clark correctly attired for a lesson in jodhpur boots, jeans, chaps, and schooling gloves. Although this helmet is acceptable for lessons and schooling for adults, I'd prefer to see her wearing a helmet with a safety harness.

manship. Along with learning to mount correctly, turn, and ride safely, you should also learn all about horses and their care. Expect to help get your horse ready for your lessons by grooming him and tacking up. After the lesson, you should cool down the horse and attend to him properly. A good rider is also a good horseman. Until you understand horses and their needs, you will not be a complete rider.

If after your first few lessons you're not enjoying yourself or are dissatisfied for any reason, talk to the manager and your instructor. Sometimes just changing groups can be a big improvement. Different stables have various specialties and philosophies. Sometimes your goals are different from what the stable has to offer. Some people work better in a highly structured environment, others learn more quickly in a casual atmosphere. Figure out your needs and state them clearly. If the stable is unable to accommodate you, shop around for a new riding academy.

After twenty lessons or so, you should know whether you want to continue on and possibly show. Many stables have schooling shows as a regular part of their lesson program. Take advantage of these to discover how you feel about showing. If your stable doesn't have schooling shows, check with your instructor for opportunities to show elsewhere. If you have a good experience at your first show and want to do it again, it's time to start focusing on your show training.

SHOW PREVIEW—GOING AS A SPECTATOR

The best way to learn about and experience horse shows is to attend them as a spectator. In this way you can decide if you want to show yourself someday. Go with a more experienced buddy who'll be able to answer your questions.

As with any other sporting event, if you don't understand what you're watching, you may be bored. Don't hesitate to ask questions of other spectators, grooms, riders, coaches, and show officials. Most are happy to answer you and explain what's going on. But use

Groom Ramona Friedley with Baltimore, taking a little rest break. (Previously appeared in HorsePlay.)

good judgment when picking a time to ask questions. Make inquiries between classes and on the lunch break, not when a rider is about to compete. There are plenty of times at a horse show when nothing is going on, so save your questions for those periods.

Start by attending a lower level, one-day show. These shows give you the opportunity to see all the divisions and classes offered in the span of one day. Get up early and arrive an hour before the show starts—observe how much time and energy goes into preparing a horse for the show ring. (Most shows have a snack booth, so you should be able to find coffee to get you going.)

Get a show program (not always available at small shows) or a class schedule. See what classes are going on in each ring. Plan to see at least part of each division, so you'll become familiar with the requirements. Make the most of your time at the show and attempt to learn as much as you can.

Horse shows are the products of many hard-working individuals.

Judge Andi Hengen marks her card with show results.

Professional course designer Laura Devendorf of Midway, Georgia, directs the building of a grand prix jumper course.

Here's who you'll see, bustling about, making things happen.

WHO'S WHO AT A HORSE SHOW

Manager — the person responsible for all organizational aspects of the show, supervising all show staff. Can be found anywhere from the parking lot to the show ring.

Judge — the individual who evaluates the competitors and horses, and then awards placements and ribbons. Usually seen sitting in the judge's stand, or standing in the ring with the horses and riders.

Ringmaster — the person who assists the judge by directing and organizing the horses and riders in the actual show ring. Usually seen in the ring with the judge.

Steward — the individual who makes sure the show runs by the rules of the governing association, and goes smoothly. She also ensures the safety aspects of the show.

Announcer — the person who announces over a p.a. system and keeps competitors informed of the show schedule. He also often helps the show secretaries figure out point standings for the championships and other such duties.

Course designer — the individual who plans and builds the courses of fences that the horses jump over.

Jump crew — the people who assist the course designer in setting up the fences and courses.

Secretary — the person responsible for checking in the competitors and collecting entry fees. She must also keep total records for competitors' placings in each class.

Gatekeeper — the individual who regulates the flow of horses into and out of the show ring.

Barn or stable manager — At multiday shows where there's overnight stabling, this person is in charge of stall assignments and security.

Horse show secretary Ann Hunt helps competitors sign up for classes at the Senator Bell Farm Horse Show in Chester, New Hampshire.

Any sporting event is more exciting if you have someone to root for. Pick a horse and rider at the beginning of the day and track their performance throughout the show. Watch everything they do closely, whether they're riding, grooming, or tacking up.

A job well done! Groom Tracy McNeil with open jumper Cantadoe.

Grooms are the heartbeat of the show world. They know horses, and can be a fountain of knowledge. Find a professional groom to talk with. Ask what has to be done to prepare a horse to show. Ask questions relating to show horse care. Perhaps she'll have some tips or secrets that would make your first show easier and more enjoyable.

The most important classes

15

for you to watch are the beginner classes. These are the ones you'll soon be competing in. Observe how the class progresses and the way riders perform. See what's required of the horses and riders. If you don't understand what's going on, ask someone to explain it to you. Who do you think are the best riders and horses? Compare your picks with the official placing.

After the riders leave the ring, find a satisfied and cheerful competitor to talk to. The best time to approach her would probably be as she's walking back to her trailer. Explain that you're thinking of showing yourself. Ask for her suggestions and thoughts on showing. Sometimes the best people to talk to are just one step ahead of you in experience. Everything will still be fresh and new to them, and they'll be able to give you a realistic perspective. If you've chosen a person who doesn't care to converse, just seek out someone else.

Spend some time watching the advanced riders and horses. These classes will be more entertaining to observe than the beginners', but may be more difficult to understand. Try to figure out what makes these people better riders and competitors. Once again, if you have any questions, ask someone to explain what's happening. Find an

Young riders competing in a flat class at the Hampton Classic Horse Show. Amanda Termini on Rocky, a Welsh pony, is in the foreground.

advanced rider to talk with and ask how long it took to get to this level of expertise.

Walk through the trailer and stabling areas. Observe how the horses are both prepared and cooled down. There are many different methods of handling horses, and you'll probably see various philosophies in action. Ask about the horses you see—their breed, age, and abilities. A reasonable set of questions might be, "How old is your horse? What breed is he? How long did it take for him to reach this level of showing?" You'll soon start to understand what horses are suitable for different levels and classes.

The show world has its own lingo and the following definitions might help you make sense of the procedures.

LINGO—SHOW TERMS

"On the flat" — equitation classes judged at the walk, trot, and canter.

"Under saddle" — hunter or pleasure classes judged at the walk, trot, and canter.

"Over fences" — any class that's contested over jumps.

"Heads up" — watch out, as in "heads up, a horse is loose."

"There is a clock on the gate" — the judge has set a time limit within which all the riders must get into the ring.

"Jump order" — the order in which riders must enter the ring for an over fences class.

"On deck" — you will be the next rider in the ring for an over fences class.

"One in the hole" — you are one away from being on deck.

"Class is closed" or **"Gate is closed"** — the show management or judge has declared that no further competitors may enter the ring for a class.

"Line up" — the judge would like you to go to the middle of the ring and stand side by side with the other competitors.

Catherine B. Knight

Jumping at the Devon Horse Show.

After you've attended a show as a spectator, consider going along with a friend who's showing. Participate in the preparation and help with the grooming. This will give you a good feel for the pressures and requirements of a show day. Plan on staying with your friend for the full day. If you find your energy flagging midway through the day, it doesn't necessarily mean that showing isn't right for you. When you show yourself, the adrenaline rush will probably perk you up and carry you through the day.

Once you've been to one small show as a spectator and another as a helper, consider attending a large, national horse show. These events showcase the talents of the best horses and riders in the country. Generally these shows run five or more days and can be quite elegant. Prize money is offered in many divisions, and competition is fierce.

Although you may never show on this level, you can still dream. Large shows are great motivators. Now, if you're excited to start showing yourself, it's time to determine if you're ready to show.

DECIDING WHEN YOU ARE READY TO SHOW

Your riding instructor mentions that there's a schooling show at your stable on Sunday, and asks if you'd like to participate. All your friends are riding in it and they're eager to share the experience with you. You're even invited to ride your favorite school horse. Should you show?

There are several important factors to take into consideration. Are you far enough along to ride safely with other people in the show ring? If you have had only private lessons and have never ridden with other horses in the ring, this is probably not the time to start. Group lessons will help you adjust to the safety issues of riding around other horses and riders. You must know the "rules of the road" before entering a show to ensure your safety and the well-being of the other riders.

Have you done your homework and attended a horse show to see how they operate? Are you *posting* consistently and confidently? Do you know your *diagonals?* The more prepared and confident you are, the more fun you'll have. Remember that having a good time should

Catherine B. Knight

A young rider, Betsy Schwartz, trotting in an equitation class on Just Another Bay, a Thoroughbred.

be the main goal. So even if you're having trouble with your diagonals, you may still want to show; however, that will decrease the possibility of getting a ribbon. If ribbons aren't important to you, and your satisfaction is found in participating, go ahead and show. Most shows have walk-trot only classes to introduce beginners to showing, and some shows have even instituted walk-trot classes where diagonals don't count, to include more riders in the show experience.

If you're a more advanced rider, ask yourself: "Is my canter seat secure and stable? Do I keep my stirrups most of the time when cantering? Am I capable of cantering in a group?" Should you feel insecure about cantering with other riders, consider walk-trot or beginner canter classes. Many shows now have beginner canter classes where the riders trot together as a group, but canter individually. Some shows even have canter classes where leads don't count, similar to the walk-trot classes in which diagonals don't matter.

Even if you're jumping cross-rails in lessons, you may want to drop down one division for your first show. It's appropriate at your first show to perform what you feel most secure doing. At a show, cross-rail riders must be capable of piloting their horses around the course without their instructor or coach in the ring. If you're not yet

Jumping cross-rails in the short stirrup division at the Hampton Classic Horse Show. Christiana Knight on Little Bits, a Welsh-Quarter Horse cross.

capable of doing this, consider riding on the flat only. It's better to be confident in a class than to struggle.

The ultimate question is: Do you really want to show? For some people showing is something they think they're supposed to do, rather than something they want to do. They see people around them excited by the prospect of showing, and think they need to join in. Examine your feelings. Are you showing to please others, or do you truly want to show? Are you excited and looking forward to showing, or are you dreading it? You should only show because you want to and because it seems like fun.

There is nothing wrong with not wanting to show. Many fine riders choose not to show. They love horses, riding, and being in the stable, but have no desire to compete. Some people ride for ten or twenty years and then suddenly decide they want to show. Others just never develop that urge.

The best time to show is when *you* feel ready and prepared. Don't be pressured by well-meaning friends or family. Showing should be an enjoyable experience. When the thought of showing elevates your mood and makes you genuinely happy—and your instructor says you're ready—then it's time to show!

FINDING A SHOW COACH

There's a difference between riding instructors and show coaches (also called trainers). Though a riding instructor can also be a show coach, and a show coach can also be a riding instructor, generally a riding instructor is a person who only teaches riding lessons. A show coach is usually someone who works only with people interested in showing. Many riding instructors don't have time in their schedules to take students to a lot of shows, whereas show coaches plan their schedules around those events.

There's no ideal way to find a show coach. In many cases the instructor you currently ride with can get you started in showing. Often, if she is experienced beyond teaching beginners, she can even take you to a few shows outside your home barn. If you plan to show only on an infrequent basis and on a casual level, your regular riding instructor may be sufficient to guide you at shows.

However, many riding instructors and coaches specialize in just a few levels of riding. If this is the case with your riding instructor, you may have to move on to someone new to advance in your riding and showing. Ask your instructor for her recommendation. Many large stables have all levels of instruction and training available. You may be able to switch to another instructor at the same barn who can train you for showing. Ask your current instructor and other people you respect for their opinions and suggestions.

In many cases, you can continue to ride with your regular instructor and take auxiliary lessons and coaching from a show trainer. When you're in the beginning stages of riding and showing, there are many skills that need practice. By availing yourself of two compatible teachers, you can accomplish a tremendous amount. Your riding basics will be strengthened, and you'll develop show ring savvy at the same time.

Show coaches should be very familiar with all aspects of riding and showing. They should either show themselves or have shown extensively in the past. Someone who has never shown can't understand the pressures, challenges, and special circumstances that complete the overall performance picture. Often, the most successful show coaches are riders who've retired from competitive showing and want to pass along their knowledge.

Working with your show coach will be different from lessons with your riding instructor. The primary mission of your riding instructor was to get you safely and happily riding a horse. The show coach will be teaching you how to show off your abilities. Riding basics will still be taught, but the emphasis will be on actual performance in the show ring.

Your show coach will teach you the customs, etiquette, and rules of safety of the show ring. Once again, don't be afraid to ask questions. "Are loud, plaid riding jackets acceptable?" (A resounding no.) "Can I wear rubber boots?" (Yes, if it's a small show.) "What happens if I fall off?" (Brush yourself off and get back on.) "What do I do if I have to go to the bathroom in the middle of a class?" (Wait.) No question is insignificant or silly.

Although it's hard to imagine, your show coach was once a beginner, too. She missed her diagonals in walk-trot classes and lost her stirrups in her first canter class. If she denies these events ever happened, she is either: a) lying, b) forgetful, or c) Katie Monahan Prudent*.

At any gathering of show riders and coaches, talk eventually turns to embarrassing things they did as beginners. One well-known rider fell off his horse onto the *judge* in his first show. Another had a stirrup and leather fall off, and galloped crying out of the class. One fell into a brush box (a wide, box-shaped jump) and got stuck with her legs sticking straight up; it took two members of the jump crew to extricate her.

The moral of all this is that nothing you can do will upset or surprise your show coach. If it does, switch to a coach with a sense of humor! Your show coach's function is to enable you to achieve your goals while helping you to keep your sanity and, as always, have fun.

(*Member of the United States Equestrian Team (USET), and one of the premier riders in the world.)

A group of child riders and their proud parents attending their first show.

CHAPTER TWO

Getting Fit

GETTING FIT FOR RIDING means exercising both the body and the mind. Here we will examine the physical exercises you can do to strengthen your body, and the mental preparation and philosophies that will make showing easier and more enjoyable.

EXERCISES FOR BEGINNERS

Riding uses muscles not tested in many other sports. The average fit person will discover this after her first lesson, when she's so sore she can barely climb off the horse. The only way to get fit for riding is to ride. However, there are exercises you can do between lessons that will help. As with any exercise plan, consult your physician before you begin.

Calf Stretches
Almost all beginner riders have trouble keeping their heels down. This is probably the most prevalent fault seen in the show ring at the beginner level. It can be caused by having either a tight Achilles tendon or

tight calf muscles. To loosen and strengthen these areas, stand with the balls of your feet on the edge of a step. Holding onto the wall or banister, gently press your heels down until you feel the stretch. Press and release twenty times, twice a day. After several weeks, you should see a difference when you're riding.

Strengthen Knee Muscles

Another common fault of beginners in the show ring is over-gripping with the calf. This causes the knee to turn out, which loosens the leg grip. When viewed from behind, you can actually see daylight between the rider's knees and the saddle. The ideal rider's leg has an equal grip between the calf, knee, and thigh. A good isometric exercise to correct an open knee is to sit on the ground with legs bent and feet flat on the floor. Place a pillow folded in half between your knees. Gently squeeze and try to press your knees together through the pillow. Repeat ten times, holding for 10–15 seconds, twice a day. This will strengthen the muscles around the knee and enable you to grip the saddle correctly.

Improve Posture

Many beginner riders have posture problems such as rounding the back, looking down, twisting the upper body, and dropping the shoulders. It's especially important with children that you have their backs checked for scoliosis (curvature of the spine) and other growth disorders. Many doctors and chiropractors routinely screen for this.

If twisting and poor posture don't have a physical cause, steps can be taken to overcome this problem. Practice good posture all the time, not just on the horse. Sit up straight and walk with your head straight and erect. Abdomen-strengthening exercises such as sit-ups are useful, as are back exercises. Yoga stretching and routine ballet exercises will also prove beneficial, as they stress posture.

There are exercises you can perform on the horse that will improve posture and balance as well. While your riding instructor has you on the lunge line, beginning at the walk, place your hands on your hips and concentrate on squaring your shoulders, raising your chin, and looking directly in front of you. After you're comfortable at the walk, move up to the trot, then canter. Once you're secure in this exercise, start again at the walk. Still on the lunge line, lean down and touch one foot at a time with the hand on the same side. Progress from there to stretching over and touching the foot on the opposite side. Repeat this at the trot and canter, if possible. This exercise will make you more aware of your body angulations and help you fix posture problems.

Practice Mounting and Dismounting

Mounting and dismounting is a test commonly asked of beginners in the show ring. A correct mount—always done from the *near* (left) side of the horse—starts by placing the reins over the horse's head and holding him by the reins under his chin. On the *near* (left) side of the horse, move your hands to midway between his ears and withers. Adjust the reins so that they're snug enough to keep the horse from walking off. If your horse tends to nip at your buttocks as you mount, shorten the *off* (right) side rein. This will flex his head outward and away from you. Now grasp the reins in your left hand only while grabbing a handful of mane. Flip the leftover loop of the reins to the off side. Face toward the off side hip of the horse with your body. Grasp the stirrup with your right hand. Place your left foot well into the stirrup. Once your foot is secure in the stirrup, point your toe into the girth so that you won't poke the horse with the toe of your boot. Place your right hand over the saddle and grasp

Hallie McEvoy

Kimberly LeMay demonstrates touching her toes.

Hallie McEvoy

the back of the off side cantle. Pull yourself up and over the horse, making sure your right leg doesn't drag over the horse's rear end. Move your right hand to the pommel of the saddle and gradually and lightly lower yourself into the saddle. Pick up your off side stirrup with your right foot. Gather the reins into both hands.

To dismount, place the reins in your left hand. Flip the rein loop to the off side of the horse. Place your right hand on the pommel. Drop your right foot out of the stirrup. Raise your body with your right hand and arm, up and over the horse, moving toward the near side. Move your leg over the back of the horse without it touching the horse. Bring your legs together and grasp the back of the saddle with your right hand. You should now be in an upright position against the near side of the horse. Kick your left foot out of the stirrup and slide lightly to the ground still holding onto the reins with your left hand. Move to the near front of the horse and bring the reins over the horse's head. Grasp the reins directly under the horse's chin with your right hand. Fold the remaining rein in half, and hold in the middle with your left hand.

Hamstring and Calf Stretches

Many people have difficulty mounting and dismounting properly due to tight hamstring and calf muscles. An exercise commonly

known as the "runner's stretch" can help with this problem. Place one heel on the floor turned slightly outward and keep your back leg straight. Lean into a wall with your other foot forward until you feel a stretch in the calf of your back leg. Hold this position for 15 seconds and repeat three times, twice a day.

Another good exercise to stretch hamstrings and make mounting easier is done lying on your back in a doorway. Lie with one leg on the wall and the other leg straight through the doorway. Move your buttocks toward the wall until you feel a stretch in the back of the thigh of the leg on the wall. As your muscles relax, move slightly closer to the wall. Repeat this exercise three times for each leg, twice a day.

Of course, if you're 4 feet 11 inches tall and your horse is 16.2 hands, you'll still have some difficulties mounting and dismounting.

Improve Hand Position

Another common show fault of beginners is having hands that are too high or stiff. A good mounted exercise to correct this can be done on the lunge line. As your instructor lunges you at the walk, relax and hang your hands at your sides. To help your hands achieve complete relaxation, shake them repeatedly as if you were shaking water off them. When they feel soft and relaxed, pick up the reins again. Imagine honey dripping through your fingertips, softening your hands and pulling them in a relaxed downward position. Repeat this exercise up through the trot and canter.

Warm-Up

As with any sport, it's important to stretch and warm up before riding to prevent muscle strain and other injuries. Many of the exercises detailed above for strengthening the body can also be used as warm-ups to stretch and tone before riding. Check with your physician or fitness trainer for other warm-up exercises. Just 5 minutes of simple stretches can save you from a sore body later on.

Feeling Fit

Sometimes being overweight can hinder your sense of feeling fit. It also makes exercising more difficult. If you've been thinking about losing a few pounds, now is the time to do it. You've already taken the positive step of riding, which is great exercise and burns a lot of calories. Now continue on and start sensibly cutting calories. Talk to your doctor about what your ideal weight is and how to achieve it. But don't wait to show until your body is "perfect," just go ahead and show. If you wait until you're happy with your fitness level and weight, you'll just keep putting it off. Use the show as a goal and motivation and have a good time.

Although riding muscles can only be developed through riding, exercise in any form is beneficial. The more fit you are physically, the easier it will be to get strong and in condition for showing and riding.

MENTAL PREPARATION—DEALING WITH PRESHOW JITTERS

Before going to your horse show, make a list of goals. These should not be earthshaking objectives, such as qualifying for the National Horse Show. They can be as simple as getting your diagonal correct or keeping your horse going at an even pace. Work with your trainer to set realistic and attainable goals. If your goals are too lofty, you're liable to suffer disappointment. If your goals are in reach, you'll be able to measure your improvement.

Mental preparation is just as important as physical preparation prior to a horse show. Your horse might be braided, your tack is clean and shiny, but you are a bundle of nerves. You can't possibly enjoy yourself if you're a nervous wreck! Some anxiety is to be expected, of course. However, if it interferes with your enjoyment or performance, you need to work on relaxing.

The positive alternative to being a nervous wreck is to possess what I call "healthy nerves." Healthy nerves are what you feel when you're really eager to show. Your horse is schooled to perfection (or as close as he gets), you feel good physically, and you're ready for the task at hand. You actually fear not performing your best, rather than suffering a general fear of failure. This nervous energy or stage fright can be useful in achieving your peak performance. Many top successful riders and athletes perform their best when they have this "nervous edge."

The biggest fear of many competitors is of embarrassing themselves. They don't fear falling off and getting injured; they fear being laughed at. This fear is irrational. There are very few people who would scoff or laugh at other competitors—and who cares what that type of person thinks of us?

A good mental exercise to get over the fear of embarrassment is the "underwear scenario." (It's a variation on the advice to imagine that everyone in the audience is in his underwear.) Imagine yourself walking into the ring wearing nothing but your underwear and singing an old show tune out of key ("Oklahoma!" works well). Everyone you know is there to watch the spectacle, including your family and your boss. Now, could anything you do in the show ring embarrass you more than that?

You can't fear what other people think of you in the show ring or in life. Fear of embarrassment stifles creativity and discourages positive action. It keeps you from enjoying yourself and from pushing your personal limits. Resolve to have a high embarrassment threshold; allow yourself to be silly, joyful, and relaxed.

Fear of getting hurt is harder to cope with. Some people with this anxiety have never been injured riding. Others have been injured and can't let go of their fear. Either way, this anxiety can interfere with your performance and pleasure. You need to examine this fear and decide if it's rational or irrational.

Rational fear is the type of anxiety that occurs when what you fear is a very real possibility. An example is fear of falling off if your horse bucks, because it has happened in the past. This is an anxiety grounded in fact. However, just because it happened before doesn't mean you're doomed to repeat the experience. Examine yourself and your horse: Has your riding improved since this accident occurred? What can you do to prevent it from occurring again? Most faults and accidents are due to the rider's error, not the horse's. Discuss the fear with your coach and work on your weak points that caused the fall the first time.

Irrational fears are the result of an overactive imagination. If you observe someone else fall, this may trigger anxiety. What specifically are you afraid of? For many people it's a particular type of jump such as an oxer or a coop. Others fear cantering in a large group. Although nothing has happened to you in the past to cause this anxiety, you're sure something horrible will in the future. The best solution for this type of fear is "desensitization." Expose yourself to the situation or object that's scaring you. You need to gain control; don't allow the situation to control your feelings and emotions. Have your instructor or coach help out. Re-create the scenario that you fear. If a particular type of jump scares you, attack it in your lessons. Start with the jump very low until you're comfortable and relaxed jumping it. Overcoming your fear may take weeks or even months. Gradually increase the height and vary the angle of approach. Be patient. Soon you'll feel comfortable and capable over this type of fence.

Situational fears, such as cantering in large groups, can also be dealt with in this manner. If you're comfortable cantering in a small group, gradually have more people join you. People are usually happy to help, because they, too, need assistance at times. Have your instructor talk to you while you're cantering with the crowd. Gradually you'll become comfortable doing what previously made you nervous.

Should you find that your nerves are still interfering with your enjoyment and performance, there are other options. Many therapists now specialize in sports psychology. These therapists work with athletes at all levels to teach them how to cope with stress and fear. Kip Rosenthal, a former top-ranked rider, combines a successful show coaching career with her sports psychology practice. Her clients include top international riders as well as beginners. She employs the latest methods in combating stress and nerves to ensure a relaxed, peak performance.

Always keep in mind that showing is supposed to be enjoyable. If you're a nervous wreck, you're either not prepared or taking it too seriously. Keep the experience in perspective; world peace will not be affected by your performance. Show, have fun, and learn something. And if you do poorly, there's always another show next weekend.

Use the following questionnaire to help determine your "Mental Horse Show Goals." Complete these sentences then take the key words you come up with to fill in the blanks and examine them. There are no right or wrong answers. Use your responses as a guide to what you need to work on. Remember, your goal should be to show, enjoy yourself, and be relaxed—all at the same time.

I wish I felt _____ when I thought about showing.

When I'm nervous, I ride _____.

My horse takes advantage of me when I feel

_____.

I wish I rode like _____.

When I fall off I feel _____.

If I don't receive a ribbon I _____.

When I don't ride well I feel _____.

When my trainer makes a suggestion I respond by

_____.

When my horse goes poorly I _____.

I fear _____ when showing.

I love _____ when showing.

I want to improve at _____.

HORSE HEALTH AND FITNESS

You might be ready to show, but is your horse? You're full of energy and eager to ride all day, but your partner looks like the star of a commercial for diet feed. Is this four-legged couch potato prepared to go to a show? Let's review the steps required for optimum horse health and fitness for showing.

Whether you own your own horse or not, you should be familiar with basic horse health requirements and ailments. Take a personal interest in the health of your favorite lesson horse. Often, riding students are able to point out changes in horse health or fitness to their instructors.

Study equine anatomy and memorize the correct terms for each body part. Learn about the most common horse ailments such as colic, laminitis, heaves, worms, and azoturia ("tying up"). Become as familiar as you can with all aspects of horses: The more you understand about their mechanics, the better a rider you'll be.

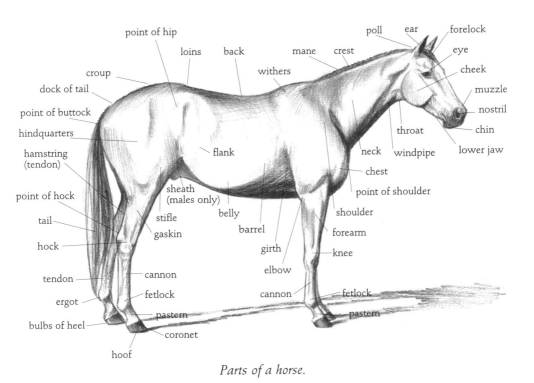

Parts of a horse.

Dr. Kevin Landau, DVM, draws blood for a Coggins test.

The most important consideration in horse health from a show-ing standpoint is being familiar with all required vaccinations. Various regions of the country require different shots. Consult with your veterinarian about his recommendations. At a minimum, he'll suggest vaccinating against tetanus (lockjaw), influenza, rhino pneu-monitis, and Eastern/Western and Venezuelan encephalitis (sleeping sickness). Some veterinarians additionally recommend vaccines for rabies, Potomac horse fever, and strangles.

Your horse will require a negative Coggins test for admission to shows. In this procedure, blood is drawn and tested for the presence of equine infectious anemia (swamp fever). Any animal testing positive must be quarantined and will not be allowed to show any where in North America. Unfortunately, there is no cure and a pos-itive carrier will remain so.

Consult your veterinarian before starting any exercise program for your horse. While he's giving your horse vaccinations, have the veterinarian perform a physical checkup. Your horse's heart, lungs, teeth, eyes, and legs should be checked for any abnormalities. Once your horse is given a clean bill of health, you may start an exercise program.

There are different levels of fitness in horses. A horse doesn't need to be "racehorse fit" to complete a walk-trot division success-fully. However, a walk-trot horse still must be fit enough to perform his job comfortably. Likewise, a horse that will compete in the Children's or Adult Amateur Hunter classes must be physically ready to jump a course of fences safely.

Just as with people, a horse must build up gradually to each new level of fitness. All exercise programs should begin with plenty of walking. After several days of increasing the time spent walking, trotting may be introduced to the schedule. After the horse has built up his trotting program, cantering and jumping can be added. Your trainer or coach can help you devise the best program for your horse.

There is no rigid rule as to the amount of time that should be spent getting a horse fit. Use common sense when planning the exercise schedule. Overweight and older horses generally take longer to regain condition. Take care not to push them too fast, as injuries might occur. Younger horses become fit quicker, but still use care to reduce the risk of strains and injuries.

Your veterinarian and your coach care about the well-being of your horse. Use them as resources to institute the best possible exercise program.

CHAPTER THREE

The Basics of Showing

THERE ARE MANY THINGS to contemplate before your first show. The *type of show* you should attend deserves serious thought. Individual *classes* need to be examined for suitability. You'll have to assemble a *show wardrobe. Show rules, regulations, etiquette,* and *customs* must be learned. *Sportsmanship* must be stressed and practiced. *Safety* measures and concerns must be reviewed. You must consider the *expenses of showing* as well. These items are all important in your show planning.

All these points can seem overwhelming to think about. So much of what happens at horse shows is specific only to showing—the rules, the wardrobe, even the customs. One important area that does carry over into daily life is sportsmanship. If you've learned the traits of good sportsmanship from your show experiences, then you've been given a lifelong gift.

The competitor to whom people are drawn is the one with the brightest outlook and with the best sportsmanship. This is the rider you'll see cheering for everyone else's jumping rounds and congratulating people when they leave the ring. If you fall off, he'll be the first to reassure you and relate a story about his tumble at another show. This is the type of person who'll go far in all endeavors, because he can motivate, socialize, and empathize with everyone. Many shows give sportsmanship awards to recognize this refreshing behavior.

To begin you on your showing journey, let's start by examining different types of shows.

TYPES OF SHOWS—SCHOOLING, OPEN, AND AHSA

There are three categories of hunter-jumper shows: schooling, open schooling, and AHSA. The type of show you compete in depends on several factors. These include your ability, the level of expertise your horse possesses, the location of the show, and your horse-showing budget. Your instructor or show coach can help clarify what show(s) will be suitable for you.

Schooling Shows

The starting point for most riders is the schooling show. Schooling shows (also called "closed" or "private schooling shows") are exactly as the name implies, a place to get educated in the art of showing. These shows are generally run by a stable exclusively for their own students. Riders use the same horses that they ride in lessons. Additionally, they usually show in the same ring that they have lessons in.

Riding a familiar horse in your own lesson ring is a low-key introduction to showing. It's not always required that the horse be braided or extensively "turned out." Often these shows do not require formal show dress, so anyone can participate. Many riders show only in schooling shows and feel no need to move on.

Schooling shows have several strong points to recommend them. They're less expensive (generally $3 to $8 per class), less stressful, more convenient, and more lighthearted than bigger shows. On the negative side, there's a low level of competition, weak judging, and a lack of sophistication. Nevertheless, schooling shows are the most sensible places for most riders to get started.

Open Schooling Shows

Open schooling shows differ from regular schooling shows in that they invite riders from other stables to participate. These shows may take place at your barn or at a neighboring stable. Either way, the level of competition is higher here. The dress code is also slightly more stringent and the horse's turnout must be better. The cost of entry into an open schooling show is slightly higher as well. Classes will generally run from $6 to $12 per class.

Open schooling shows are sometimes referred to as "unrecognized" shows, meaning they are not recognized by the AHSA. However, this does not mean that they may not be affiliated with another organization, such as state or regional horse show organizations that keep a record of points won by competitors, and then give year-end awards.

This type of show is also a good place to get started. Although the rider might be in strange surroundings, he'll probably be on a familiar horse. Most lesson horses have been to more than a few schooling shows in their day. They know the ropes and are great assets to beginning show riders.

Many stables even have a series of open schooling shows at their location, or have a series of shows in conjunction with other barns. These series may offer year-end championships and prizes in addition to individual show awards. Show series are a good introduction to more intense competition with structured goals to work toward.

AHSA (Recognized) Shows

AHSA (also called "recognized") shows are the highest level of competition for a recreational rider. Riders from a wide geographic area attend these shows and the competition is fierce. The dress standards are high and professional horse turnout is expected. The caliber of mounts is far above your average lesson horse. (This is not to disparage lesson horses; on the contrary, many lesson horses are wise, older, retired show horses that can no longer handle the physical demands of constant showing.)

These shows are conducted by individual show managements under the jurisdiction of the AHSA. The AHSA sets the rules and guidelines for everything from the judge's qualifications to the type of recordkeeping required. These guidelines ensure a quality horse show and specify consequences if a show is not run in accordance with regulations.

In order to enter an AHSA show, you must be a member or pay the nonmember's fee. A class at an AHSA show costs from $10 to over $75, for members and nonmembers alike.

AHSA shows are divided into categories by rating, and the cost varies with the rating of the show and the prize money offered. The largest and most prestigious shows are rated A-3, and these shows offer the most prize money, the highest level of competition, and generally the most points for year-end awards. The other show ratings in descending order are A-2, A-1, B, C, and Local.

Year-end awards are presented nationally and by region, and are divided into the different categories of *hunters, hunter seat equitation,* and *jumpers.* Presently, there are no AHSA annual awards for the *pleasure division* within the hunter and jumper framework. (There are many annual pleasure awards in other divisions such as Western, Morgan, and Arabian.) Each division is then further divided by style, level of expertise, quality, and height of fences. For instance, within the hunter division are 1st Year Green Hunters, Amateur Owner Hunters, Junior Hunters, Small-Medium-Large Pony Hunters, Conformation Hunters, and many more.

As a rule, AHSA shows are *not* the best place to start showing, because of the expense and effort involved in having a polished turnout, as well as the higher stress level for riders, trainers, and show personnel. Unless you're exceedingly secure in your riding and have the utmost faith in your horse, it's wise to begin at a schooling show.

The exceptions to this are the smaller, "Local"-rated AHSA shows. Many of the Local-rated shows include extra classes for beginners and advanced beginners. Although the expense is still greater than for a schooling show, these Local-rated shows offer a solid beginner experience. In addition, participants are assured of a quality show with professional officials. AHSA Local-rated shows offer the best of both worlds.

Discuss your showing goals and concerns with your instructor. Together you can make the best decision as to where you should start showing. No matter what type of show you choose, learn the requirements and rules of each class and division. Again, don't be afraid to ask what may seem to you like silly questions. All questions have merit. Once you've decided what show will be your first, it's time to pick some suitable classes.

TYPES OF CLASSES AND CLASS REQUIREMENTS

There are four principal divisions at most hunter-jumper shows. They are *equitation, hunters, jumpers,* and *pleasure.* Each division has many different classes (or events). The division or divisions you choose to ride in depend on several factors, including your level of ability, age, confidence, horse's talents, and instructor's approval.

Your instructor's approval is especially important. If your instructor says you're not ready for a specific division or class, trust her judgment. You're paying for her expert advice, so it behooves you to heed it. Her concerns are for your safety, comfort, and well-being. It's far better to enter a lower division and be safe than to compete in an insecure manner. Very often riders will listen to their egos rather than to common sense, and the results can be disastrous.

Catherine B. Knight

Christiana Knight trots Clean Sweep in an Equitation Class.

Equitation Division

Equitation classes are judged on the rider's position, horsemanship, poise, and ability "on the flat"* and over fences. The manner in which the horse moves does not count. The exception to this is if the horse is out of control or moving incorrectly due to rider error. At the trot, diagonals count heavily, as do proper leads at the canter. The judge is looking

"On the flat" refers to equitation classes that are judged at the walk, trot, and canter. Hunter or pleasure classes judged at the walk, trot, and canter are referred to as "under saddle."

for riders who most closely conform to the picture of good horsemanship and position.

The most common equitation fault of beginner riders is weak position. This includes heels up (toes down), loose legs, sitting behind or ahead of the motion, having a rounded back, looking down, and high or rough hands. Other common equitation faults are wrong diagonals, wrong leads, poor steering, and bad balance.

What the Judge Looks for in Equitation Classes

- Correct leg position
- Proper upper body position and posture
- Good hand position and effectiveness
- Overall control (steering) and horsemanship
- Correct leads and diagonals
- Organization and planning
- Promptness to respond to commands
- Ring savvy and common sense
- A neat and attractive appearance
- Meeting the fences at the correct "spots," meaning jumping the fences from the best place to take off

---

Hunter Division

Hunter classes are judged on the horse's movement, presence, brilliance, manner of going, overall quality, and jumping ability. Hunters are judged over fences and under saddle (walk, trot, canter, and sometimes hand gallop). The rider is not judged at all, unless something he does interferes with the horse's performance.

The ideal hunter under saddle has a low, long, ground-covering stride with little excess movement (what horsemen refer to as a "good mover"). He is expected to be mannerly, pleasant, and go in a well-balanced frame. Hunters over fences must maintain a steady pace, meet their jumps neatly on even strides, and jump in good form. Any deviations from these ideals will result in a lower placing.

Many horses are suitable for hunters but not equitation, and vice

Catherine B. Knight

Sara Marcus showing Primo Ré, a buckskin Quarter Horse, in a hunter class.

What the Judge Looks for in a Hunter

- ↻ The horse's jumping performance and talent
- ↻ Attitude
- ↻ Soundness and good movement
- ↻ Overall quality of the horse
- ↻ Safety of the horse's jumping style
- ↻ Suitability of the horse for the rider
- ↻ Straight lines and approaches to fences
- ↻ Even pace
- ↻ Meeting the fences cleanly and neatly (on stride)
- ↻ Good manners
- ↻ Correct leads
- ↻ Attractiveness of the horse
- ↻ Conformation (in certain classes)

versa. Some equitation horses are not great movers or jumpers, but are steady and honest and present their riders well. Many good hunters are difficult to equitate on because they have such big movement and incredibly athletic jumping styles. It's hard to do an "equitation pose" on a horse who jumps big and really uses his body. It's easier to ride equitation on a horse who jumps a little "flat."

Jumper Division

Jumper classes are judged on *faults* and *time*, over fences only. The rider's and horse's form are not considered. The standard is cut and dried: You either have the fastest clean round (meaning one without faults) or you don't. Riders must be able to maneuver their steeds deftly and quickly around tight turns and over fences.

There are different parameters in each jumping class. Some are judged on *touches* and *time*, others are judged on *faults* and *time*. There's a *time allowed* and a *time limit* for each course. The *time allowed* is the time in which you must complete the course without receiving penalty points. The *time limit* is the time in which you must finish the course or be eliminated.

Faults are penalties for errors. Rails that are knocked down are scored as four faults. Refusals are scored as three faults for the first refusal and six faults for the second refusal. The third refusal results in elimination. Going off course and jumping the fences in the wrong order also result in immediate elimination. In a *touch class*, in addition to the jumping penalties described above, touching the jump with the front or hind legs will result in an additional one or half fault.

Many people enjoy competing in the jumper division because there's little room for subjectivity on the part of the judge. Riders may not have perfect position, and their horses may not be pretty jumpers; however, they're extremely talented riders with athletic horses. The jumper division allows them to show off their talents.

The jumper division is the only one of the four divisions discussed here that's offered on an international level. It's this division in which riders on the jumper squad of the United States Equestrian Team compete. The jumping style of the USET members is what all serious hunter-jumper riders aspire to.

What the Judge Looks for in a Jumper Class
- The fastest clean round
- No faults (refusals, knockdowns, or exceeding the time allowed)
- In a touch class, faults are added for the touch of a fence with the horse's body or legs
- Ability to follow course

Pleasure Division

Pleasure classes are judged under saddle only. They're similar to hunter classes in that they're judged based on the horse's performance. However, the qualities the judge looks for are slightly different. A successful pleasure horse doesn't have to be the best mover in the world, but he should move evenly and willingly. A pleasure horse must be quiet, safe, and obedient. Above all, he should be—as the term implies—a pleasure to ride.

Many horses who don't have the brilliance or movement of a hunter make wonderful pleasure horses. They move in a steady manner with good pace and have agreeable personalities. Lesson horses tend to do quite well in pleasure divisions because of their quiet natures and even temperaments.

What the Judge Looks for in a Pleasure Horse
- Manners (the most important)
- Obedience
- Willingness
- Soundness and even movement
- Travels in straight lines
- Correct leads
- Suitability for the rider
- Safety (carries his rider safely and quietly)

Catherine B. Knight

Christiana Knight had a successful day on Little Bits, a Welsh-Quarter Horse cross.

Almost all riders start out in the equitation, hunter, and pleasure divisions. Many then advance to the jumper division, which takes more technical skill and daring. Some riders choose to specialize in either equitation or hunters; many do both. Explore all the options. Compete in the divisions that you and your horse are best suited for, and choose classes that you enjoy.

Sample Classes in Each Division

Note: A rider's age for showing purposes is her age as of the previous December 1.

Note: Not every class listed is offered by every show. Many shows offer different or additional classes that fit their purpose or clientele.

EQUITATION

- **Walk/Trot Equitation:** an equitation class judged only at the walk and trot.
- **Beginner Equitation:** open to riders who have never won a ribbon.
- **Maiden Equitation:** open to riders who have never won a blue ribbon.

- **Novice Equitation:** open to riders who have not won three blue ribbons.
- **Limit Equitation:** open to riders who have not won six blue ribbons.
- **Open Equitation:** open to all riders. Riders are not limited in the number of ribbons they have won.*
- **Short Stirrup Equitation:** generally, open to riders ages 12 and under.**
- **Long Stirrup Equitation:** classes for adult riders (18 years and older).
- **Children's Equitation:** open to children 17 and under.
- **Adult Equitation:** open to all adults. This class is sometimes broken down into different age groups, such as 18 to 35 years old, and 36 and older.

HUNTERS

- **Short Stirrup Hunter:** hunter classes for riders 12 years of age and under. Fence height is usually 18" or cross-rail size.
- **Children's Hunter Horse or Pony:** open to riders ages 17 and under. Generally, horses jump 2'6" to 3' and ponies jump 2' to 2'6".
- **Pre–Children's Hunter:** a division to help prepare riders for Children's Hunters. Fence height is usually 2'3".
- **Pony Hunter:** hunter classes for ponies only, to be ridden by riders 17 and under. Generally divided into Small (12.2 hands and under), Medium (12.2 to 13.2 hands), and Large (13.2 to 14.2 hands) ponies.
- **Junior Hunter:** hunter classes for horses, to be ridden by riders 17 and under. Usually divided into Large Junior Hunter (16 hands and over) and Small Junior Hunter (14.2 to 16 hands).
- **Maiden Hunter:** hunter classes open to horses and ponies who have never won a blue ribbon in a hunter class.
- **Baby Green Hunter:** open to horses and ponies who have

---

* *Includes AHSA Medal and ASPCA Maclay*
** *For horse show purposes, your age for the showing year is however old you are on December 1 of the previous year.*

never shown over fences prior to the current year. Fence height is generally 2' to 2'3".

☞ **Low Hunter:** open to horses and ponies. Fence height is usually 3'.

☞ **Pre–Green Hunter:** hunter classes open to horses who have never jumped 3'6" or over. Fence height is usually 3'.

☞ **Adult Amateur Hunter:** hunter classes for adult riders who are amateurs. Fence height is usually 2'6" to 3'. Classes are sometimes divided into age groups of 18 to 35; 36 to 45; and 46 and over.

☞ **Amateur Owner Hunter:** hunter classes for amateur riders who own the horse they show. Fence height is 3'6". Classes are sometimes divided into age groups of 18 to 35, and 36 and over.

☞ **1st Year Green Hunter:** open to horses of any age in their first year of showing at recognized competitions. Shown over fences of 3'6".

☞ **2nd Year Green:** open to horses of any age in their second year of showing at recognized competitions. Shown over fences of 3'9".

☞ **Regular Working Hunter:** open to all horses, not restricted by previous showing or winnings in any division. Shown over fences of 4'.

☞ **Conformation Hunters:** open to the same horses that show in 1st and 2nd Year Green, as well as in the Regular Working Hunter Division. In addition to being judged on their jumping ability and movement, they're also judged on their conformation.

☞ **Side-Saddle Hunter:** a hunter class in which ladies ride sidesaddle. Shown over fences of 3'.

JUMPERS

☞ **Open Jumpers:** open to all horses, not restricted by previous winnings. Fence height is 4' to 5'3", with spreads of 4' to 6'.

☞ **Schooling Jumpers:** open to all horses. Fence height is 3'6", with spreads up to 3'6".

- **Preliminary Jumpers:** open to horses who have won less than $2,500 in jumper classes, or in their first year of showing in jumper classes. Fence heights range from 3'9" to 4'6", with spreads of 3'9" to 5'.
- **Adult Amateur Jumpers:** jumper classes open only to riders 18 and over who are amateurs. Fence height is 3' to 3'6".
- **Children's Jumpers:** jumper classes open only to riders 17 and under. Fence height is 3' to 3'6".
- **Junior/Amateur Owner Jumpers:** jumper classes open to riders 17 years of age and under or adults who are amateur riders on their own horses. Fence height is 3'6" to 4'6", with spreads up to 5'.
- **Pony Jumpers:** jumper classes for ponies 14.2 hands and under. These classes are no longer found at many shows.
- **Puddle Jumpers:** beginner jumper classes where the fence height is very low.

PLEASURE

- **Open Pleasure:** open to all horses and ponies, not restricted by previous winnings.
- **Pony or Horse Pleasure:** a pleasure class open to either ponies or horses.
- **Adult Pleasure:** a pleasure class for riders 18 and over.
- **Children's or Junior Pleasure:** a pleasure class for riders 17 and under.
- **Walk/Trot Pleasure:** a pleasure class that is only judged at the walk and trot.
- **Bridle Path Hack:** a pleasure class in which the horse is asked to hand gallop and back, in addition to walk, trot, and canter work.
- **Hunter Pleasure:** a pleasure class in which the horse's suitability to be a hunter-type horse is also considered.
- **Hunter Hack:** a class in which horses first perform at the walk, trot, and canter. They are then asked to jump two small fences, no more than 2'6" in height.
- **Trail Class:** a class contested over real and simulated obsta-

cles that might be found on a trail. Examples of this include opening and shutting a gate, retrieving mail from a mailbox, and carrying a raincoat, all while mounted.

SHOW CLOTHING AND FASHIONS

The three most frequently asked questions of a horse show judge are:

1) What did I do wrong?
2) Where is the bathroom?
3) Do show clothes make a difference in how a judge views a class?

Question number 1 can be answered only on the individual rider's level, and only after the rider receives permission to address the judge. The second question varies according to the show grounds. The final question has no simple answer.

When an official is judging an equitation class, he's trying to pick the best rider. A competitor who has taken the time to attend to every detail of his appearance has generally also practiced and is well schooled. His performance reflects his meticulous preparation on every level; he's ready to show. An attractive turnout may give a rider an edge in the general overview of the class, but it shouldn't cloud the judge's assessment as to who deserves a ribbon. Elegant, expensive attire won't serve as a substitute for form, talent, and horsemanship.

Although showing is not a fashion competition, it has its own traditional code for dress. Planning your "riding habit," as the standard uniform is called, should be viewed in the same way as dressing for business or a night on the town. A certain dress code is required. At the large national shows, the dress is extremely formal. Certain classes, such as *Hunter Classics,* require top hats and shadbelly coats, in addition to the standard boots and breeches. At the regional and state levels, the customary dress of boots, breeches, specialized shirt, riding jacket, and safety helmet suffices. In schooling shows and other lower levels of showing, the dress code is a bit more flexible. In beginner classes, the judge is more concerned with safety in riding gear than fashion. Most judges make allowances for beginner riders in turnout. It's important for beginner competitors to enjoy the show experience and be enthusiastic about continuing on, and many riders simply don't have the wherewithal to purchase complete outfits the first few times they show. It's common to see competitors in paddock boots, tan pants or jeans, a polo shirt, and a safety helmet. These riders should be judged on their performance and not their turnout.

However, there are certain safety and fashion rules that must never be broken, even for beginners. Sneakers, shorts, and T-shirts are *never* acceptable. Footwear must have a stiff sole with a heel, pants have to be ankle length, and shirts should be polo or Oxford in style. Although AHSA shows allow adult riders to show in a helmet without a safety harness, it's not a good idea. A proper helmet with safety harness is one of the best precautions a rider can take against possible head injury.

When outfitting yourself to show, be practical. Riding clothing need not be brand new or expensive to be suitable for showing. Fit, comfort, and cleanliness are the three most important considera-

Hallie McEvoy

Kimberly LeMay wearing a well-fit safety helmet with harness.

tions. Try to borrow clothing for your first show or make do with the best you have. Some people show once and never show again, so don't overspend on your first outing. Many tack stores and thrift shops include a section of used riding clothing, often priced very reasonably.

Here's a rundown of the standard elements of proper turnout.

Helmet

The most important piece of show clothing is the safety helmet. Head protection is the one area in which you must not cut corners. Any helmet you wear should be American Society for Testing and Materials (ASTM) and Safety Equipment Institute (SEI) tested and approved. It must have a sturdy safety harness and it must fit well. Correct fitting of a riding helmet should be done by an experienced tack shop employee or riding instructor. Depending on the shape of your head, the helmet should sit midway on your forehead between your hairline and your eyes and fit snugly. Riding helmets generally cost between $35 and $150, depending on the features and materials. Most experts advise that once a helmet has sustained severe impact in a fall, it should be replaced. It's believed that the safety qualities of the helmet shell are compromised with any impact. Although this replacement can be expensive, it's still cheaper than the consequences of a bad, unprotected fall.

Women and girls whose hair shows outside the helmet should wear hairnets to restrain flyaway locks. Hairnets can be purchased at most drugstores for under a dollar. Girls who are twelve years of age or younger who are showing ponies may wear pigtails.

Women should not wear earrings other than small studs that won't get tangled with the helmet's harness or the hairnet. It's extremely painful and distracting to have an earring ripped off while riding.

Boots

The boots you use for riding lessons can probably be worn at your first show. Even if the boots are rubber, they're suitable for your show debut. There's no sense in spending a lot of money on boots until you're sure showing is something you want to do more of. If you continue to show, leather boots will be a must for both comfort and fashion. Rubber boots cost from $25 to $50; leather boots range from

Field boot (left) and dress boot (right).

$50 up to $400 for those that are custom made.

There are two basic types of tall leather boots. The first is the field boot, which has laces on the instep that improve the comfort and fit of the boot and make it easier to pull on and take off. Acceptable colors for show field boots are black and shades of brown. The second type of boot is the dress boot. Dress boots are smooth and plain at the ankles and don't have laces. The preferred color for dress boots is black. Both field and dress boots may have spur rests, swagger tabs, or extra-high tops.

Boots should come all the way up to your kneecap for proper fit. Riding boots that are too short give a disjointed look to the leg. They should give good support to the arch of the foot and fit snugly the whole length of the calf. Boots should be comfortable for both riding and walking.

Breeches

Breeches (pronounced *britch-es*) are riding pants that are designed to be worn with high boots. They should be close-fitting and are suitable to show in as long as they're beige, gray, tan, or rust. Canary (yellow) is also an acceptable color, but it has gotten very hard to find breeches in this tone. Many beginner riders have one pair of breeches that they use for their lessons. These will usually do the job for the first couple shows. The wild tones that breeches can now be found in, such as purple or shocking pink, are not allowable unless it's a very small, in-stable schooling show. Breeches cost from $25 all the way up to $300 for imported, European brands.

A belt should always be worn with breeches or jodhpurs, as it completes the picture. Belts should be made of good-quality leather or cloth and may be solid, braided, or tastefully decorated. There's probably a suitable one hanging in your closet. If not, belts may be purchased at the tack store for $15 to $100.

Jodhpurs, Jodhpur Boots, and Paddock Boots

It once was common to see adult riders wearing jodhpur pants and paddock or jodhpur boots at shows. This style has fallen out of fash-

Kimberly correctly attired in jodhpurs, paddock boots, and jodhpur straps.

Kimberly, at 13 years old, is at the age and height where she is ready to wear tall boots. Here she is correctly and elegantly attired for showing in field boots, breeches, ratcatcher, choker with pin, gloves, and a safety helmet with harness.

ion in the past twenty years. Most adults prefer the support that tall boots give to their legs and ankles. However, jodhpur pants and boots *should* be worn by most riders twelve years of age and under, depending on their height and size. It's not suitable for very young riders to wear tall boots and breeches, because the tall boots prevent the child from developing a proper leg and feel for the horse. Jodhpur boots and pants are much more practical and elegant for young riders.

Jodhpur pants are close-fitting and come to the ankle. They must be worn with leather knee straps, which keep the jodhpurs from twisting, and elastic boot straps, which keep them from riding up on the leg. Jodhpur pants cost $25 to $100. Paddock boots (which lace up) and jodhpur boots (which have no laces, but elastic panels or

Jodhpur boot (left), paddock boot (center), and trotter boot (right).

zippers that allow them to be pulled on) come just above the ankle. They run from $25 for synthetic leather to $350 for a custom-fit boot with top-grain leather.

Shirts

Riding shirts worn by women are sometimes referred to as *rat catchers*. These are shirts that button all the way up to the middle of the neck and have no collar. A ratcatcher will come with a solid choker collar that covers the top buttons. Solid pale colors or pin striped patterns work best with most riding jackets. The variety of riding shirts has increased in recent years. Brighter colors and patterns are now commonplace in the show ring.

A stock or choker pin can be used to hold the collar to the shirt and provide a touch of elegance. Other people choose to have their chokers monogrammed and don't use pins. Many people are uncomfortable and concerned about the safety of having a pin right next to their throat. If a pin is worn, it should be small and under-stated with a strong clasp. Gold and silver are both acceptable. Prices range from $5 up to thousands of dollars for jewel-encrusted pieces.

Most men wear solid or pinstriped Oxford-style shirts with a con-trasting tie. Ties should be conservative and a tie clip or tack should

A ratcatcher with collar and stock pin (left) is standard for women. An Oxford-style shirt with tie (right) is standard for men.

be used, so that the tie doesn't fly loose. The cost of a suitable riding shirt is $20 to $100.

Jackets

Riding jackets should be comfortable and provide a trim, neat appearance. For correct fit, the sleeves should be long enough to cover your wrist bone when standing with arms relaxed at your sides. You should also be able to squat or kneel and stretch your arms forward without feeling undue pull under your arms or across your back. Riding jackets are often sized differently from regular jackets, as many come from Great Britain where clothes are measured by a different system. Check with tack shop personnel for the best fit. Prices range from $50 for a basic jacket to $800 for a custom-made wool coat.

The preferred tones for riding jackets in hunter seat shows are all dark, conservative colors. Navy blue, hunter green, and dark gray, either pinstriped or solid, are the best picks. Some subdued plaids and checks may also work. Remember to match the jacket with the shirt. There's a wide range of materials available to choose from. Wool, cotton, and other natural blends tend to be more comfortable and "breathe" better than synthetic coats.

Gloves

Gloves complete the picture. Colors worn should be tan, brown, dark brown, or black. Some people like to match their gloves to their boot color; others like to contrast it. Gloves can hide a multitude of hand problems—always an important consideration for a beginner. Prices start under $10 for "Isotoner"-style gloves, and range up to $100 for fine, imported Italian kidskin gloves.

Additional Tips for Show Turnout

Several fashion tips that sometimes are neglected can help finish your appearance the day of the show. Velvet and velveteen helmet coverings often get flat or matted spots from storage. These can be steamed out over a boiling teakettle. Hold the helmet and rotate it through the steam, being careful not to scald yourself. Use masking or duct tape to pick lint off your jacket, rather than buying an expensive brush. Last, when at the show, rub your boots with a damp cloth after mounting to remove dirt and dust.

At horse shows, the classic and timeless hunter seat outfit is black boots, beige breeches, white shirt, and navy blue jacket. You can't go wrong by being conservative. Styles come and go, but understated and quiet elegance will always be in fashion. The show ring is not the place for fashion experimentation.

Show clothes must be functional and comfortable. An outfit is useless if it looks great but is so tight you can't move. Conversely, you can't present a neat appearance if the riding jacket is too big and the boots are too short. Stay within your budget while buying the best quality you can afford. Remember, it's only a horse show. Don't invest a large sum until you're sure showing is for you.

SPORTSMANSHIP, ETIQUETTE, AND
HORSE SHOW CUSTOMS

If there were an advice column for horses to consult—a horsey "Miss Manners"—a common letter would read as follows:

Dear Prissy Pony,

My rider has very poor manners. When she wins a ribbon at a show, she never nods and thanks the ringmaster. She also whines that her placement should have been higher. Some days, she even blames me for her performance, or lack thereof. I would buck her off, but I fear she would fail to make the connection. How can I teach her to be polite?

Signed: Apple Dumpling

Dear Apple,

Go right ahead and buck her off! There's no excuse for ungrateful behavior toward you or the human show officials. If she's really as negative as you say, her fellow competitors will cheer to see her fly through the air. Toss her gently so as not to harm anything but her pride. Perhaps this experience will set her straight.

All my love, Prissy Pony

There are many points of show etiquette that aren't listed in any rule book. Most are based on the straightforward premise of good manners. It is hoped that you will bring the same gentle manners you employ at work and school to your recreational show activities.

Ask your instructor, other horsemen, and friends who show about horse show etiquette and its traditions. Although some customs may seem overly formal, they're part of show ring tradition. These traditions add to the mystique and lore of showing.

Sportsmanship

Perhaps the most basic tradition of the show ring is sportsmanship. Good sportsmanship is expected of competitors at all times. No matter how large or small the event, there's no room for poor behavior. The ability to win or lose gracefully is an important quality in all sporting events, and in life in general.

This tongue-in-cheek sign hangs in the show secretary's office at Fred's Farm in Chatham, New York. It reads:

> Horse Show Ethics
> 1) Prod the Announcer
> 2) Heckle the Judge
> 3) Hassle the Staff
> "Let's get the damn show moving along!"

"Horse Show Ethics" sign at Fred's Farm in Chatham, New York.

Hallie McEvoy

Unfortunately, some people actually behave in this manner. Nothing is accomplished by poor sportsmanship, but that doesn't stop some from excelling at it. A horse show should not be an arena for cutthroat competition. It's expected that riders practice good sportsmanship. But spouses and parents of competitors should behave with decorum, too. (A parent who cheers on a rider to fulfill his own fantasies is a victim of what I call "Little League syndrome.") Good sportsmanship should be practiced in any competition.

The Sportsman's Charter from the AHSA Rule Book states:

> That sport is something done for the fun of doing it and
> that it ceases to be sport when it becomes a business
> only, something done for what there is in it;
> That amateurism is something of the heart and spirit—
> not a matter of exact technical qualifications;
> That good manners of sport are fundamentally important;
> That the code must be strictly upheld;
> That the whole structure of sport is not only preserved
> from the absurdity of undue importance, but is justified
> by a kind of romance which animates it, and by the
> positive virtues of courage, patience, good temper, and
> unselfishness which are demanded by the code;
> That the exploitation of sport for profit alone kills the spir-
> it and retains only the husk and semblance of the
> thing;
> That the qualities of frankness, courage, and sincerity
> which mark the good sportsman in private life shall
> mark the discussions of his interests at a show.

So how can you keep sportsmanship and fun in the show experience? The best way is to remember that it's just a horse show. Keep this in perspective at all times. No matter what the outcome of the show, it will not affect the rest of mankind.

Little things can make the difference in sportsmanship. One nice touch is to write thank-you notes to the show management and secretary after the show. Many show managers and secretaries are volunteers, and a thank-you note shows your appreciation of them. Always be kind to workers on the grounds, whether they're members of the jump crew or food concessionaires. There will be a day when you may be performing their same functions, and you'll want to be treated with respect.

Should you have a problem at the show, try to handle it gracefully with sportsmanship in mind. Don't whine, shout, or curse. No problem is ever solved by bad behavior. Enlist the help of your trainer and the show steward, if necessary, to resolve a crisis. Most problems stem from poor communication, so choose your words carefully. Kindness and respect always go a long way to smoothing a difficult situation.

Acknowledging the Judge and Ringmaster

Specific etiquette and customs in the show ring include the polite procedure for receiving a ribbon. A man is expected to remove his helmet when accepting a ribbon. A boy should nod and touch the peak of his helmet when accepting a ribbon. (Riders seventeen years of age and under are not allowed to remove their helmets while mounted on the show grounds.) He should then express thanks to the ringmaster. Women and girls should nod their heads and express their gratitude. Some people take it one step further and dismount to accept their ribbons. A smile is correct in any circumstance.

Another show ring custom that's important to be aware of is the correct procedure for excusing yourself from the ring in the event of a problem. Should you find yourself with broken tack or horse trouble that would necessitate leaving the ring, you must ask the judge's permission to be excused. You may do this by asking verbally; or you may nod and tip your hat to the judge. This indicates that you wish to leave the ring. Never leave the ring without first asking permission—it's considered poor form to do so.

Follow Instructions

Tradition says that you follow the ringmaster's directions. Although no specific rule commands this, it's understood that you will. The ringmaster takes his direction from the judge, so by ignoring him you show disrespect for the judge. This can often be seen when a class is starting. Competitors will disregard the ringmaster's call to enter the ring to spend more time with their coach. This is rude and slows the pace of the show. Riders who frequently indulge in this behavior are not looked upon with favor by the judge.

It's also bad form to slow the pace at the end of a class when the competitors are called in to line up. Many riders will take an extra turn around the ring to try to get the judge to look at them one last time. However, if the judge wanted additional opportunities to observe anyone in the class, she would not have asked the ringmaster for a lineup. Respond promptly to any directions you're given.

Dress

Tradition also finds its way into the fashion of showing. As mentioned earlier, it's customary that riders be properly attired (see pages 52-59) in show clothing, unless it's a small schooling show. Although traditional show clothing is attractive, some elements may not be the most practical choices. Breeches and boots make sense from the viewpoint of safety and comfort. The breeches give you sufficient stretch and movement to ride correctly, and boots support your ankles and protect your legs from rubs.

On the other hand, riding jackets and shirts ("ratcatchers") with stiff chokers are not sensible for comfort or flexibility. It would make greater sense to wear softer, more durable and flexible fabric. However, jackets and ratcatchers are customary, and have their origins in the sport of foxhunting.

When foxhunting, riders would wear tailored jackets and high-collared shirts with a "stock tie" over them. From a fashion standpoint, it looked very attractive. The reason for the tie, however, was that it could be unwound and used as a bandage for an injured horse or rider. This tradition has found its way into the modern show ring. Although most riders no longer wear stock ties, they do wear the choker-style collar with their shirts and tailored jackets.

A stock tie is still worn for foxhunting.

List of No-No's That Can Be Seen at Many Shows

- Riders who yell at their coaches, spouses, or parents.
- Riders who throw their ribbons on the ground upon leaving the ring.
- Riders who refuse to accept a ribbon because it's not the one they wanted.
- Riders who blame the horse every time they don't receive a ribbon.
- Competitors and coaches who blame the judge when they don't receive a ribbon.
- Riders who ignore the ringmaster's call to enter the ring or lineup.
- Parents who pressure their children to win.
- Children who pressure their parents for a better or more talented horse, when it's their riding that needs improvement.
- Competitors who complain over minor inconveniences.
- Competitors who "forget" to correctly fill out entry blanks.
- Competitors who forget their manners.

RULES AND REGULATIONS

The rules and regulations of horse showing can seem overwhelming to learn and confusing to understand. There are good reasons why most rules were instituted, based on safety and humane considerations and in the interest of streamlining procedures.

The various organizations do have rules that differ slightly from one another. However, as a hunter-jumper rider, the rules that will apply to you are written by the American Horse Shows Association. If you plan to show more than once a year at AHSA shows, you should join the organization. The *AHSA Rule Book* specifies procedures and rules for competitors, and you're expected to be familiar with them. (The *AHSA Rule Book* is also useful when you can't get to sleep the night before a show; by the time you wade through Chapter 10, Title 12, Section 2, Level 4, Subsection 29, Paragraph 30, you'll be feeling very sleepy.)

The following rules apply to AHSA shows only, but are a good guide to correct behavior at any show. These are in no way a complete guide to AHSA rules and regulations, but rather an introduction to the rules that most affect beginners.

Don't Ask the Judge What You Did Wrong

As a beginner at horse shows, your initial reaction after a class might be to ask the judge directly what you did wrong. This is strictly prohibited by the rules. There are two important reasons for this. First, it helps keep the judge from being harassed and influenced by disgruntled competitors. Second, if everyone asked the judge's opinion, the show would be slowed down to a crawl. If you feel you *must* speak to the judge, ask the show steward (clearance from the FBI would also be helpful). The steward will then approach the judge for her permission. Remember to speak respectfully and don't waste the judge's time. No rider may look at the judge's cards without the judge's permission.

Behave Politely

A regulation that must be obeyed faithfully regards polite behavior. It's a shame that a rule actually had to be instituted to control lack of sportsmanship. You can be fined for publicly disparaging the reputation of a show official. This includes remarks about the show official's parentage, eyesight, and fairness. This rule is to uphold the official's integrity and the reputation of the AHSA. Infractions of good sportsmanship are taken seriously. If you do have a grievous fault with an official, ask the show steward for a report form to send to the AHSA. These complaints are investigated, so be sure that your claim will withstand scrutiny.

Regarding the "Courtesy Fence"

One rule affects the way classes over fences are run. Up until 1996, you were allowed to remount after a jumping fall and jump a "courtesy fence." The thinking was that you should get back on and jump at least one fence for confidence. It was up to the judge whether a courtesy fence would be permitted. Now, if you fall, go off course, or have more than three refusals, you must leave the ring immediately, due to liability and safety concerns. The reasoning is that if you've demonstrated an inability to ride the course, you should not risk a courtesy fence. If this courtesy fence were allowed and the rider injured, it's feared that this could be used as an excuse to sue the horse show or the judge. Once again, because of the litigious times we live in, a rule had to be passed to protect horse shows and officials.

Helmets with Safety Harnesses Are a Must

Riding helmets with safety harness fastened are expected of all junior riders (show ages seventeen and under) when mounted on the show grounds. This rule has saved many riders from severe head injuries. Adults may wear a helmet without a safety harness, but a safety harness is still strongly recommended.

The Use of Gag Bits

Humane considerations are the backbone of many rules. Many such regulations apply to the type of equipment that's recommended. Certain tack and bits are considered too harsh for showing in particular classes and are frowned upon by judges in those classes. An example of these is the gag bit, a type of bit that uses leverage and pressure on the horse's mouth and the poll of his head. Gag bits are openly allowed in most jumper classes, but not recommended for equitation and hunter classes, where they're considered nonconventional and too extreme. The rule book recommends the use of regulation snaffles, pelhams, and full bridles in hunter and equitation classes.

Training Practices Are Regulated

"Poling" is a practice that is strictly regulated because of humane concerns. Poling occurs in the schooling area. A pole is used to "rap" the horse's front legs as he jumps. The thinking behind this is that it will make the horse jump cleaner. I don't like it, but for many it's an accepted training practice. The rules specifically spell out how poling may be done and the type of pole that may be used on the show grounds. Poling is prohibited in California.

Equipment Regulations

The rule book expressly forbids some equipment in certain classes. Martingales are an example of this. They're an allowable piece of equipment in both equitation and hunter classes over fences, but are forbidden in on the flat and under saddle classes.

The rule book also makes recommendations as to the type of equipment that's desirable. In hunter and equitation classes, it recommends standard cavesson nose bands, and specifies that a judge may penalize nonconventional nose bands. Examples of a nonconventional nose bands are drop, flash, and figure 8 nose bands, which fasten over the bridge of the horse's nose and then around the horse's lips, just below the bit. They're designed to prevent the horse from opening his mouth to play with the bit. Many horses in jumper classes can be seen wearing drop nose bands where their use is not penalized.

Putting a Clock on the Gate

Regulations designed to streamline shows include "putting a clock on the gate." This phrase means that you have a specified amount of time to get into the ring for your class. This is done only when people drag their heels about entering the ring or the show is on a tight schedule. A rider may want to wait for her trainer, or may be too casual about getting to a class on time. Either way, when many people start acting in this manner, the pace of the show is slowed down. Shows must finish within a certain amount of time after starting. Hence, officials have no choice but to do something to move the show along.

The show management or judge may then put a clock on the gate and announce the amount of time in which people must enter the ring. If a rider doesn't get there in time, the "gate is closed," and she forfeits the class. Although this may seem harsh, it's necessary to keep shows running on time. It's the rider's job to be ready and prepared to show, and this includes getting to the class promptly.

Show rules and regulations have evolved over the past one hundred years. All rules have a solid reason for their existence, whether it be for safety, prevention of cruelty, or administrative purposes.

Please familiarize yourself with the rule book(s) of any organization you'll be showing under. Ask your instructor or coach to clarify any points you find confusing.

SAFETY AT HORSE SHOWS

The general rules of horse safety and common sense are even more important at shows. The old schooling horse who has never done more than a grudging trot at home may turn into Secretariat when brought to a show. The adult who's always level-headed may panic when faced with a safety issue that normally wouldn't cause a second thought. The capable child may freeze when a horse bucks, and not be able to remedy the problem.

The best way to ensure that none of these situations occurs is to see that all safety rules are well rehearsed at lessons. When you're at a show with a bad case of nerves, safety measures must be ingrained to be effective. A safety response should be automatic, as there's no time to waste. Seconds may make the difference between an injury and just a good scare. Instructors and students must rehearse worst-case scenarios to prepare for emergencies.

Helmets

As explained, a good riding helmet is a necessary piece of safety equipment. Your brain must be protected at all times. Many instructors require that their students wear helmets to groom and lead horses, not just for riding lessons. Countless people have been saved by their helmets during riding and grooming accidents. Even if you're "just going for a short ride," wear your helmet. For people who are concerned that helmets mess up their hair, there's a saying commonly heard in stables: "People who think their hairdos are more important than their brains are probably right."

Vests

Safety vests for jumping and riding have gained popularity in recent years. These vests are padded across the chest, back, and shoulder areas. Combined-training riders must wear them to help cushion inevitable falls. They're comfortable and should be worn for beginner through advanced lessons over fences. It's optional whether to wear a vest for a lesson on the flat, but it certainly couldn't hurt. These vests cost between $125 and $200.

Leading

At a horse show, the most common accidents occur when a rider is leading the horse. As you lead your mount, keep well away from unfamiliar horses. This is a good idea for two reasons. First, allowing your horse to mingle with strange horses is courting disaster. Your horse may take dislike to another horse on first sight. If you let these two horses get close, anything from kicking to biting is apt to occur. The second point is that unknown horses can carry diseases. If you allow your horse to "socialize" and smell the other horse, you're inviting germs to make themselves at home in your horse.

To lead your mount correctly, place yourself on the near (left) side of the horse. The reins should be brought over the horse's head. Hold the end of the rein loop in your left hand, while your right hand grasps the reins under the horse's chin. You should face forward in the direction you wish to proceed. Place yourself midway between the horse's nose and shoulders, about 1 to 2 feet away from the horse. This leaves you close enough to control the horse, but far enough away that your toes won't be trod upon. Motivate the horse to move by tugging gently forward on the reins. Reinforce this with voice commands, saying, "Walk." Steering is accomplished by pushing or pulling the horse's head gently in the direction you want to go.

Trailering

Horses are transported to and from shows by horse trailers or vans. Loading and unloading a horse can be dangerous. Have your trainer show you the safest method for your particular make of trailer. Ramp loading is slightly different from step-up trailers in how you approach the task. The most common loading injuries to humans are stepped-on toes and bruised ribs from getting "squished" by the horse. Until you're comfortable and secure with your horse's actions and personality, have an expert take care of the loading and unloading.

Loading a horse into a trailer takes experience.

If in between classes you tie your horse to the trailer, make sure he's never left alone. Horses occasionally panic when tied, and the consequences can be grave. Tie a loop of baling twine to the trailer, then tie a slip knot to that. If the horse frantically pulls back, either you can unhitch the slip knot or the baling twine will break, thereby releasing the horse. Make sure you're well away from the hind end of the horse when he's pulling back; when the baling twine snaps, he may fly back suddenly.

Grooming and Tacking Up

When saddling and bridling at a show, take extra precautions. A horse that normally stands quietly may toss his head when being bridled. For this reason never stand directly in front of the horse when bridling or grooming. More than one person has had his nose broken by a horse's head toss. When saddling, make sure the horse is aware that you're at his side with a saddle. Some horses get so preoccupied with all the show activity that they don't realize that you're next to them. A horse may spook and pull away in this situation. It can be quite embarrassing to be running after your loose, half-tacked horse.

Loose Horse

One of the most dangerous situations at a horse show is when there's a loose horse running through the grounds. Try to alert the show announcer to warn everyone in the vicinity. Generally the announcer will say, "Heads up, everybody—loose horse on the grounds!" As a beginner, don't try to be a hero by flinging yourself in front of the careening horse. Stand back and let more experienced horsemen catch the animal. The exception to this rule is if you know the horse very, very well, and know how he will react.

Falls

When you're riding in a show class and a rider falls off and his horse gets loose, stop and stand your horse quietly. Some horses get excited when they see a riderless horse zooming about in an enclosed ring, so be prepared for your horse possibly to "act up." If this occurs and you don't feel capable enough to handle it, dismount quickly and hold your horse in hand. There's no shame in acting safely. Have your instructor teach you how to do a "flying dismount" for emergency situations like this.

Should you be the unfortunate rider who has parted company with your horse, get up as quickly as possible if you aren't injured. Catch your horse and remount as soon as you can, so as not to delay the class. If you are hurt, indicate to the ringmaster or judge that you require assistance. Very often, you'll have the wind knocked out of you, but you'll feel better in a few minutes. Everyone who shows eventually falls off in the ring, and there's no disgrace in doing so.

Keeping a Safe Distance

While riding in the show ring, keep as much distance as possible between yourself and the other competitors. A good rule of thumb is to stay at least two horse lengths apart. In small, crowded rings this is difficult, but try to stay separate as much as possible. If you find yourself riding up too close to someone, check your path, cut across the ring, and find an open slot. During the final lineup, try to find a large open spot to stand alone. At either end of the line is generally the safest place to park.

Riders correctly spaced in a lineup.

Kicking

Any horse with a red ribbon tied in his tail is a kicker. The red ribbon is the universal "scarlet letter" for kickers. Needless to say, avoid getting anywhere near this horse. In the lineup at the end of the class, *do not* pull in next to him.

Dogs

Dogs and horse shows can be a dangerous combination. Although it seems like such a perfect environment for a dog (sunshine and fresh horse manure to investigate), it can instead be perilous. Should a dog run into the ring while a class is in progress, tragedy is possible. Horses spook, riders fall off, and dogs get stepped on. Dogs should be left at home; if one is brought to the show, he should be restrained at all times. Young children, too, must be watched with extreme vigilance.

Friends and Family

Your friends and family will want to attend the horse show and watch you ride. Make sure you explain to them the unpredictable nature of horses. Teach them the basic rules of behavior around horses so they won't be in harm's way. Explain that they should never walk up directly behind a horse, as they may be kicked. Do not allow them to hang over the ring fence or sit on it, as they might frighten a horse. Warn them to be careful around horses with their cameras, as many horses are afraid of the flash and whir. Should a child want a "pony ride," have her wear a safety helmet even if it's "only for a minute."

"NEVERS"

Never walk up behind a horse; always approach from the side or front.

Never shout or run around horses.

Never leave children unsupervised around horses.

Never touch a horse that you don't know.

Never tie a horse directly to a trailer; always use a loop of baling twine tied to the trailer.

Never ride without a safety helmet.

Never allow friends or family to ride without a safety helmet.

Never allow a strange horse to touch noses with your horse.

Never crowd another horse as you are riding or leading.

With proper safety precautions, your first shows will be memorable and injury-free. When in doubt about what constitutes safe behavior, check with your coach or instructor.

EXPENSES OF SHOWING

Showing is expensive, even on a casual level. There's the cost of the horse himself, as well as tack, clothing, lessons, board, shoeing, veterinarian, vitamins, worming, trailering, show and membership fees. Even if you don't own a horse, there are still lease fees, clothing, lessons, and show fees. Either way, showing can be costly—but worth every penny!

I love horse shows. Whether I'm judging, competing, or watching, I get an amazing amount of enjoyment from them. Yes, the expenses of showing may be hard to justify to your accountant, but that's true of many other sports. Court time for tennis can be $25 to $50 an hour. Ice skating requires lessons and many pairs of costly skates. A day ticket for skiing is about $35, and that doesn't include lessons or rental equipment. When put in perspective, riding and showing are not that outlandishly priced.

For the recreational rider who only shows once or twice a year at schooling shows, the expense can be moderate. If you don't own a horse, leasing a horse from your stable will run anywhere from $5 per class to a $100 fee for the day. Coaching the day of the show will cost between $10 and $100. Schooling show entry fees range from $3 to $12 per class, depending on the size and scope of the show. All told, for non–horse owners, it's easy to spend anywhere from $35 to $250 on a simple schooling show, and this doesn't take show clothing into account.

The average amount spend by non–horse owners is probably about $50 to $100 per show. Is this too much to spend for a wonderful day of fun, competition, and horses? That's up to you. I know many people who scrimp and save to go to a few horse shows a year because it brings them so much pleasure. They skip going out to dinner, they clip coupons, and they make do with the clothing they have so that they can show. Their victories are all the sweeter because of the sacrifices they've made.

For horse owners, of course, the costs are greater. Unrelated to showing, there's board, or feed and labor if you keep the horse in your backyard. Board can cost anywhere from $150 to $900 a month, depending on the location of the stable and the services it offers. Shoeing runs approximately $40 to $100 every six to eight weeks. A physical, Coggins test, and routine vaccinations from the veterinarian cost about $75 to $150 once or twice a year. Additional visits by the veterinarian for injuries and sickness can add up.

Lessons and show coaching cost $10 to $100 a day. Trailering to horse shows will cost anywhere from $1 to $3 a loaded mile. Entry fees will range from a low of $3 for a schooling show class, to over $75 for a single class at a recognized show. Membership fees for the

AHSA and regional or local organizations can easily add up to $200 a year.

How do people afford horses and showing? Many work at second jobs. Some get support from family or spouses. Others work at the stable to offset the cost of board and services. It's not always easy, but people who want to show find a way for it to happen.

Many of the top riders in this country weren't born into wealthy families that could afford unlimited showing. Margie Goldstein-Engle, the crowd-pleasing Grand Prix rider, worked hard to get where she is. Through will and determination she made her way up the horse show ladder. She exercised and rode horses for other people, mucked out stalls, and did whatever she had to do to show. Her efforts have led her to where she is today—one of the top jumper riders in the world.

If you want to ride and show but you can't afford it, see if you can work off lessons and showing at your stable. Jane Savoie, the famous dressage rider, once said, "If you can dream it, you can do it." Go out and find a way to make your showing dreams happen.

CHAPTER FOUR

Horse Show Preparation

HORSE SHOW PREPARATION can be hectic and confusing. There are entry forms to fill out, horses to bathe and braid, tack to clean, and trailering arrangements to make. All this may seem daunting, but with a bit of foresight and organization it can all go smoothly.

You need to cope with preshow jitters (see pages 31–34) and tackle the chores ahead of you. With the right attitude, your first shows can be stress-free and enjoyable. Whether you receive a ribbon or not, showing should enrich your riding and your life. Undue stress needn't be part of the day.

The key to good show preparation is to have a plan. Sit down with your coach and make a list of what you'll need and what must be done. This plan should allow for flexibility. Flexibility is required in all dealings with horses—they're living creatures that get ill, go lame, and have "off" days, just as we do. The weather can be capricious and force you to change your schedule. Relaxed flexibility is the best route.

People have different preparation and work styles. Some like to make a list to work from so they can check off chores as they get them done. Others like to "wing it." Whichever style works best for you, you'll need to allow enough time for each task.

Let's prepare to show.

FILLING OUT ENTRY FORMS

Entry forms are a necessary evil in the world of showing. Competitors don't like to fill them out and often do a poor job of it. Show secretaries have trouble understanding what people have written and consequently garble the information. It's gotten so bad that some shows now offer prizes for the best-filled-out entry blank!

Entry forms come as part of the prize list (also called a show or class list). You'll often see shows advertised in newspapers, in magazines, or on flyers at the stable or the feed or tack store. The show secretary's telephone number and address are usually listed. In order to receive a prize list, call the secretary and ask her to mail one to you. Entry forms are used by the secretary to enter you and your horse into the classes you've indicated.

Many shows specify the date that entries close for a show. Even if there isn't a closing date, it's a good idea to mail in your entry form at least a week prior to the show. This gives the show secretary ample time to perform her chores. Most shows request payment with the entry form, or a deposit. If you can't attend the show because you or your horse is ill, most shows will refund your entry fees if you provide a physician's or veterinarian's note.

Should you have a problem in filling out the form, call the secretary so she can answer questions for you. It's easier for a secretary to help you the week before the show, rather than that morning.

Let's examine some entry blanks. Individual shows require different information to satisfy their bookkeeping requirements for affiliation with the organizations such as the AHSA. On the next page are typical entry forms.

Note that there are spaces to record name, address, telephone number, age of competitor, horse's information (age, color, height), classes and divisions entered, money enclosed, relevant AHSA numbers, and signatures of the owner, trainer, and rider. If the competitor is a minor, the parent or guardian must also sign. This information seems straightforward enough, but very often competitors neglect to complete the form correctly. This information is required by the AHSA to track and record competitors and their accomplishments.

Fieldholm Farms Horse Show

Saturday, August 24, 1996
CLOSING DATE: August 22, 1996
COMPLETE INFORMATION IS REQUIRED FOR ALL CLASSES.

ONE HORSE PER ENTRY FORM PLEASE

For advance entries call or mail to:
Pat Medeiros
593 East Road
Tiverton, RI 02878
(401) 624-3070 or (401) 625-1330

Exhibitor Number

NAME OF HORSE	AHSA #	COLOR	SEX	HEIGHT	AGE	PONY

PONY: ☐ SM ☐ MED ☐ LG

All exhibitors must present their current AHSA membership card and pony measurement card before a horse show number is issued.

RIDER'S NAME — JR'S AGE — AHSA #

AMATEUR: ☐ YES ☐ NO

PONY MEASUREMENT CARD #

ADDRESS — ASPCA #

☐ 18 - 35 ☐ OVER 35

NAME OF TRAINER/INSTRUCTOR

CITY/STATE/ZIP CODE — USET #

Exhibitors are responsible for their own errors and those of their agents in the preparation of entry blanks.

Class Numbers Horse										Total Class Entry Fees
Entry Fee										
Class Numbers Equitation										Total Equitation Entry Fees
Entry Fee										

SIGNATURES REQUIRED IN THREE (3) PLACES (AT X) BELOW
Entries Not Signed Will Not Be Accepted -- Carefully Read This Agreement Before Signing!

Every entry at a recognized competition shall constitute an agreement and affirmation that all participants (which include without limitation, the owner, lessee, trainer, manager, agent, coach, driver, rider, handler and the horse), for themselves, their principals, representatives, employees and agents: (1) shall be subject to the constitution and rules of the association and the local rules of the competition; (2) represent that every horse, rider, driver and handler is eligible as entered; (3) agree to be bound by the constitution and rules of the AHSA and of the competition, and will accept as final the decision of the hearing committee on any question arising under said rules, and agree to hold the competition, the AHSA, their officials, directors and employees harmless for any action taken; (4) agree that as a condition of entry, they authorize the AHSA and/or the competition management to market, transfer, assign or otherwise make use of any photographs, likenesses, films, broadcasts, cablecasts, audiotapes taken of the horse(s) and participant(s) while on the grounds, incident to, or in transit between the stabling facility and the event site, in any way they see fit for the promotion, coverage or benefit of the event, sport, or the AHSA, without compensation to any of them, so long as the use neither jeopardizes amateur status nor endorses a specific product or service, and hereby expressively and irrevocably waive and release any rights in connection with such use, including any claim to invasion of privacy, right of publicity, or to misappropriation; and (5) agree that they participate voluntarily in the competition fully aware that horse sports and the competition involve inherent dangerous risk of serious injury or death, and by participating they expressly assume any and all risks of injury or loss, and they agree to indemnify and hold the AHSA, the competition and their officials, directors, employees and agents harmless from and against all claims including for any injury or loss suffered during or in connection with competition, whether or not such claim, injury or loss resulted, directly or indirectly, from the negligent acts or omissions of said officials, directors, employees or agents of the AHSA or competition. The construction and application of AHSA rules are governed by the State of New York, and any action instituted against the AHSA must be filed in New York State. See article 1502.5.

X _____ Rider's, Driver's, or Handler's Signature
(Parent/Guardian, if under 18, or if not available, trainer must sign)

Print Name: _____
Street: _____
City/St/Zip: _____
Telephone: _____
Rider/Driver/Handler's AHSA #: _____
Social Security #: _____

X _____ Trainer's Signature

Print Name: _____
Street: _____
City/St/Zip: _____
Telephone: _____
Trainer's AHSA #: _____
Social Security #: _____

X _____ Owner's or Agent's Signature

Print Name: _____
Street: _____
City/St/Zip: _____
Telephone: _____
Owner's AHSA #: _____
Agent's AHSA #: _____
Social Security #: _____

Total Class *Horse* Entry Fees	
Total Class *Equitation* Entry Fees	
AHSA Drug Test Fee @ $5.00 and AHSA Fee @ $1.00	6.00
RIHA Fee @ $2.00	2.00
Number Fee @ $1.00	1.00
Warm-Ups: $10.00 First/$5.00 Each add.	
Post Entry Fee @ $5.00	
Stall Fee @ $20.00/Day	
TOTAL	
Credit Vouchers	
BALANCE DUE	

NO NUMBERS WILL BE PICKED UP WITHOUT AN OPEN CHECK OR PAYMENT IN FULL

UNPAID CHARGES: A service charge of $20.00 per check will be levied for non-negotiable checks. All managers of future shows shall be notified of indebtedness; points shall not count for unpaid entries or at any show following and exhibitor will not be eligible for year-end awards. Any exhibitor leaving the show with unpaid entry fees will be billed and assessed a $10.00 billing fee.

Make Checks Payable To: **Fieldholm Farms**

Typical AHSA show entry form.

Senator Bell Farm Hunter Show

#

September 22, 1996

All classes are $10.00 unless otherwise stated

ENTRY FORM (Please **PRINT**) — **Pre-Entries Close: Friday September 20, 1996 !!**

Classes	Name of Horse	Pony ☐small ☐medium ☐large	Rider / Owner (indicate R,O, or R/O if same)	Total Fees

Classes	Equitation / Rider's Name		Age (**Jr. Riders give age** Adult Riders= A)	Total Fees

I hereby enter the above at my own risk, subject to the rules of Senator Bell Farm, Inc. and I hereby engage to be responsible for any injury or damages that may occur to or be caused by any animals, vehicles, or trappings, or the loss of any animal, vehicle or trappings exhibited by me, and I further agree to be absolutely responsible for the physical condition of any animal under my control or ownership and will also release, indemnify and save harmless the said Horse Show, Senator Bell Farm Inc., N.E.H.C., N.H.H.&J.A., and/or N.H.H.&T.A. from any damage, expense, and/or liability arising out of or resulting from any act or omission of the Exhibitor or Senator Bell Farm, Inc. or their agents, servants, or employees, and certify that all my Horses are free from contagious disease.

Total Entry Fees	
Warm-Up(s)	
Post Entry Fee*	
NHH&TA Fee	$ 1.50
Number Deposit	$ 1.00
Total Fees	

X _____ Rider's Signature (Parent or Guardian for riders under 21)

X _____ Owner's or Agent's Signature

Name of Rider _____
Street _____
City & State _____ Zip _____
Phone ( ) _____

Name of Owner _____
Street _____
City & State _____ Zip _____
Phone ( ) _____

Make checks payable to:
Senator Bell Farm
Mail Entries to:
Ann Hunt
172 Mountain Rd.
Weare, N.H. 03281

* **Entries close Friday September 22nd. Post entries will be charged a fee of $10 for the day.**
Refunds of entry fees will not be made unless a veterinarian or doctor's certificate of lameness, injury or illness is shown. Refunds will be made if a class is cancelled.

Typical schooling show entry form.

AHSA stewards assist show secretaries to ensure that forms are correctly and completely filled out. Some competitors who aren't AHSA members try to avoid paying the non-members fee by lying on the entry form. A competitor who lists fake AHSA numbers or other false information is fined by the AHSA. He won't be able to compete at another AHSA show until his fine is paid. In this age of computer tracking, it's easy for the AHSA to ferret out fraudulent numbers.

Many entry forms have spaces for other organizations' information, such as membership numbers. Often you'll fill out regional, state, or local organization membership information, as well as the standard AHSA information. Try to keep your membership cards in an accessible location; you'll want to find your membership numbers when you need them. A good trick is to photocopy all your cards and numbers onto a single sheet of paper. Keep this sheet in your wallet or show file.

Schooling shows generally have less complicated entry forms. Required will be name, address, telephone number, horse's information, classes entered, and payment information.

It's important to fill out schooling show entry forms carefully. Print neatly. Sloppy handwriting is the bane of every show secretary's existence. It's everyone's responsibility to ensure that a show runs smoothly, including the competitors'. The less work you make for the show secretary, the more time he has for more important chores (like announcing that he's found a pony; would someone please claim it).

PREPARING THE HORSE—BATHING, BRUSHING, AND BRAIDING

For many people, the joy of showing occurs prior to the event. There's something deeply satisfying about bathing, brushing, and braiding (the three B's) a horse. Will Rogers once said, "The outside of the horse is good for the inside of the man." In an almost magical way, your stress and worries fall away as you groom your horse.

For showing, your horse must be bathed and braided the day before the event. However, there are a few exceptions to this rule.

You can skip the bath if it's below 60 degrees and you don't have a heated wash stall. If the show you plan to attend is a small, in-house schooling show, braiding is probably not required. In all other cases, plan on bathing and braiding.

If you have never bathed a horse, ask your instructor for direction. You'll need a bucket, a large sponge, horse shampoo, sweat scraper, a hose, and towels. A horse cooler or antisweat sheet is necessary on cool days. Use warm water for bathing and rinsing. Follow the directions on the shampoo bottle for how much soap is necessary.

Many horses are fussy at bath time; two people may be required to bathe them. One person should hold the lead line and control the horse; the other then washes and rinses the horse. Start by wetting the horse down from the legs upward. Wet the horse from just behind the ears all the way to the tail. Once the horse is thoroughly wet, apply the shampoo. Scrub and work the shampoo into the coat. Don't neglect the mane and tail.

Wash the face with a warm washcloth. Take special care around the eyes, nose, mouth, and ears. Soap is usually not required on the face. If the face is very dirty and does require soap, be especially diligent about getting all of it off.

Rinse the horse completely so that no soap remains on the body. Any soap that's left will cause dry skin and itching. If you'd like, you can now apply coat conditioners or a liniment. Some products must be rinsed out, others may be left in to benefit the coat and skin. After the final rinse, use your sweat scraper to remove excess water from the coat. Rub the horse down with dry towels. Finally, put a cooler on the horse to guard against chills.

A quick note here: Horses *love* to roll in dirt when they're wet. It's a throwback to when they had to disguise their smells from predators. Don't turn your horse out in a muddy paddock after bathing—you'll have to bathe him all over again. Hand walk or graze your horse as he dries.

Once the horse is dry, brush him thoroughly. There are numerous topical applications of shine and conditioning agents that can be applied at this time. Think twice about applying them to the mane or tail if you'll be braiding. They can make the hair so slick that you won't be able to braid. Also, don't apply any product to the saddle area; it may cause the saddle to slide back.

If your horse needs clipping and trimming, now would be the appropriate time to do it. Check his muzzle, ears, and fetlocks for long hairs. These should be trimmed. Some horses object to the sound of the clippers, so you'll have to trim them with scissors. Be very careful handling the scissors around the horse, as it's easy to slip and clip something you shouldn't. If your horse requires a full body clip, enlist the aid of a knowledgeable person. A badly clipped coat will take a long time to grow in.

Hoof dressing can be applied after bathing, but you'll need to reapply it at the show. Certain compounds condition the hoof and help stimulate growth. Other preparations are merely for looks; they'll only dye or shine the hooves. Check the label for ingredients and recommendations for use.

Mane-braiding supplies required include a mane pulling comb, hair clips, braiding bands, yarn, scissors, needle and thread, and a "pull-through" (similar to a crochet hook). A wet mane is easier to braid than a dry one, so a spray bottle filled with water is helpful. Just spray and comb the area you're working on to make it more

manageable. Short manes are much easier to braid than long ones. Consult with your instructor as to the correct length of mane. Manes must be "pulled" and not cut, or the hair won't look natural.

There are several different styles of braids that are used for shows. The type of braid you choose depends on the show you're attending. For small schooling shows, braiding with rubber bands is acceptable.

Basic braiding supplies include thread, rubber bands, mane separator, mane comb, braid "ripper," braiding needles, and mane holder.

Hallie McEvoy

Braiding bands are available at tack shops for about $2. Grab about an inch's width of hair. Starting at the top of the mane at the bridlepath, divide it into three strands and braid to the bottom. Tie it off with a braiding band. Take this braid and fold it under, forming

Braiding with rubber bands.

Braiding with yarn. Professional braider, Mandy Satriano, prepares Just Another Bay for the Hampton Classic.

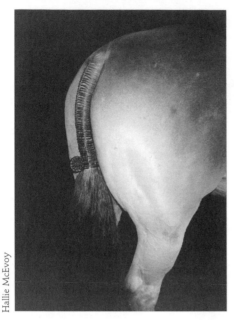

Hallie McEvoy

A beautifully braided tail with pinwheel.

a loop. Attach it to the top of the braid with another band.

For larger schooling shows and lower-rated AHSA shows, mane braiding must be done with yarn. The yarn should be the same color as the horse's mane or a quietly contrasting shade. No bright or unusual colors, please. In preparation for braiding, cut strands of yarn about 10 inches to 12 inches long. Start braiding in the same manner as above. Once the braid is started, incorporate the yarn. The loop of the yarn should go into the braid with the ends hanging down. The two yarn strands are then braided in with different hair strands. When you reach the bottom, tie off the braid by making a simple loop knot with the two pieces of yarn. Fold the lower part of the braid under the upper. Using a pull-through, pull the yarn strings up through the braid. Bring the strings behind the braid and then to the front, tying neatly. Cut off the excess pieces of yarn.

For the biggest and most prestigious shows, braids are actually "sewn in" with a needle and thread. Many grooms make their living in this specialized field of braiding. The grooms will braid all night long before a show, braiding as many as ten to fifteen horses. These braids are works of art and add glamour to the horse's overall appearance.

Tail braiding is usually not required for schooling or small AHSA shows. For larger shows, a modified French braid is used to dress up the tail. Horses with particularly ample rumps look nice with their tails braided. It adds a delicate and refined touch to their appearance.

All braids should be taken out right after the show. Braids that are left in can cause the hair to break and other damage. They also become itchy for the horse, causing him to rub and pull out the hair.

After you've removed the braids, comb out the mane and tail.

Should you be in doubt as to whether braiding is required for a specific show, be conservative and braid. It's better to be on the safe side. Braiding is considered a tradition in the show ring, and it's politely expected that you and your horse honor show ring traditions.

CLEANING AND POLISHING TACK

Competitors want to know if the style of saddle they ride in will matter at a horse show. The condition of your tack is more important than its make. The most expensive Hermès saddle can look terrible if it has not been treated well. Conversely, an inexpensive Argentine-made saddle can be very attractive if it has been consistently conditioned and well oiled. The best saddle for you to ride in is one that's supple, suits your frame, fits your horse, and is balanced and comfortable.

Dry, hard tack will be uncomfortable for both you and your horse. Tack that has been neglected is also dangerous, as it can rip or break at crucial moments. All leather should be carefully examined before you use it. Don't use tack that's cracking, peeling, or splitting. You don't want a stirrup leather to break in the middle of a class.

Bridles and saddles should be wiped down with a damp cloth after every use. This removes sweat and dirt, which attack and corrode leather. Frequently used tack should be thoroughly cleaned with saddle soap at least once a week. At this time, check whether the leather needs a conditioning treatment of oil. Neatsfoot oil is an excellent product. It replenishes the oil that the leather loses from heavy usage.

Bits must be cleaned after every ride. Simply dunk the bit into a bucket of water and wipe clean. It's not necessary to remove the bit from the bridle. Bits that are not cleaned end up with a film of "gunk" over them, especially at the end of the mouthpiece. This is uncomfortable for the horse and may cause "bit sores" on the corners of his mouth.

To prepare and polish a bridle properly for show, you must take it apart. This is time consuming, but the results are worth it. After separating the bridle, clean and condition each leather piece. Then use a leather polish to make the bridle gleam. Different polishes can be purchased at the local tack shop. Be careful while cleaning the reins—too much oil and polish may make them too slippery. Use a metal cleaner to remove dirt from the buckles and shine them up. You can sterilize the bit in boiling water. (Once when I was boiling several bits, my husband thought I was making soup. We now refer to bits being boiled as "bit soup.") Any remaining dirt or stains on the bit can be removed with a toothbrush and toothpaste.

Putting a bridle back together is like doing a jigsaw puzzle. The first time it's hard to figure out how the pieces go. Should you have trouble, ask your instructor to help.

Saddles are easier to clean and polish than are bridles; there aren't as many parts. Remove the stirrups and leathers. Thoroughly clean the saddle, leathers, and girth with saddle soap. Make sure that you clean the underside of the saddle as well. Condition and oil if necessary. Polish may be applied to the saddle, but go lightly over the seat. Too much polish in this area and you'll slide all over. Check the stirrup leathers for signs of wear, as they're pressure points when

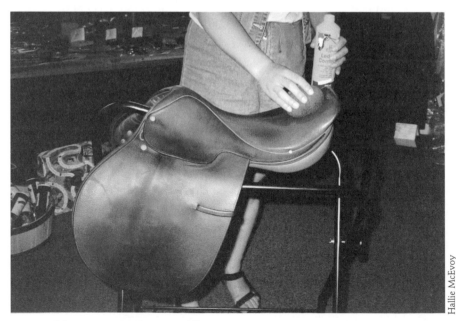

Hallie McEvoy

Be careful not to over-oil your saddle's seat.

Hallie McEvoy

Three types of bounce pads.

riding. The stirrups can be cleaned with a metal polish.

Don't forget to wash and bleach the saddle pad. White is the best color for hunter-jumper shows. Make sure the pad fits the saddle well and that there isn't an excess of saddle pad hanging out. If your saddle has an additional, or "bounce," pad (also called a "banjo" pad), be sure that it, too, is clean. There are now saddle pads that come with a bounce pad enclosed inside. These present a neater picture and work well with many saddles.

Clean and well-conditioned tack is a joy to ride and show in. It shows off your horse and riding to the best advantage. Dull, dirty tack generally indicates that the competitor did not care enough to prepare properly for the show. Always take the time to ready your tack.

TRAILERING ARRANGEMENTS AND PREPARING THE HORSE TO SHIP

Getting your horse to a show can be an adventure in itself. If you don't own a truck and trailer, you'll need to hire someone to ship your horse. Often the stable or your riding instructor will be available to provide horse transportation. Many stables own large vans that can carry ten horses at once. Unless shipping is included in your boarding contract or showing arrangements at the stable, expect to pay for the service.

Some stables hire outside, specialized shippers to transport the horses to a show. Such companies can be found in the Yellow Pages of the telephone book under "Horse Transportation," "Livestock Transportation," or "Horse Shipping." If you need to arrange your own horse transportation, check with friends, riding instructors, and tack shop employees for their recommendations. Always talk to the van or trailer driver and make sure that he has had plenty of experience in vanning and caring for horses.

Most people drive themselves, their children, and their equipment to the horse show at the same time the van leaves. Many stables even run informal car pools for everyone attending the show. They follow the van, so everyone will be there when the horses and ponies are unloaded. Following the van is also a good safety measure—if anything goes wrong in shipping, you're right there to help.

Most small shows don't have stabling on grounds for horses trailering in. This means that you'll need to work out of your car and the van or trailer. Have your equipment and tack organized neatly so that it will be easy to find what you need. While you're grooming and tacking up, keep your horse well away from the car. Open car doors and trunks are a hazard.

Many multiday shows have stalls available for overnight or daylong stays. If you're lucky enough to have stabling where you're showing, check the stall carefully. Look for anything that might be dangerous—nails, broken boards, uneven footing. A horse is more likely to injure himself in an unfamiliar environment.

Proper preparation of your horse for shipping involves several steps. First, look the horse over and make sure he's ready to go to the show. If he has thrown a shoe and cut his leg, it's better to find out before you truck him a hundred miles.

When the horse is ready to go, his legs need to be protectively wrapped. You should learn wrapping from a qualified horseman. A poorly wrapped leg can cause damage to the ligaments and muscles. Ask your instructor to show you the safest, best method of wrapping.

Most people wrap for shipping with standing wraps and quilts. This protects the area under the knee down to the fetlock. This type of bandage provides padding and support to the leg. You can also purchase shipping wraps that have Velcro closures and are simple to use.

The coronary band and bulbs of the heel can be protected with bell boots. Bell boots are circular and made of rubber, leather, or fabric. They can be pulled on or fastened with Velcro or buckles. Bell boots are good protection when many horses are crowded together, as they tend to step on one another's feet.

Head bumpers (also called head guards) are useful for horses who are high-headed or rear. Bumpers are usually made from leather padded with fleece or fabric. They fit through the halter and go over the horse's ears. They do look a bit funny, but they're an effective safety device.

Basic shipping supplies, including velcro shipping wraps, head bumper, standing wraps, tail wrap, quilts, and two styles of bell boots.

Pavarotti correctly prepared for shipping. He is wearing a head bumper, leather halter, blanket, standing wraps, quilts, and bellboots on his front legs, velcro shipping wraps on his hind legs, and a tail wrap.

Hallie McEvoy

A tail properly wrapped for trailering.

Tails should be wrapped from the top of the tail to the base of the tailbone. This ensures that the horse won't rub out tail hairs in the trailer. Many horses love to rub their tails and rumps on the bars that hold them in the trailer stalls. This tail rubbing can ruin a beautiful braiding job.

Depending on how drafty the trailer is, you may want to blanket your horse. Consider the temperature and the length of the trip. Trips on windy days with the temperature in the 70s may require a sheet or blanket for your horse's comfort. Talk with your veterinarian and other horsemen for their recommendations on blanketing.

As mentioned on pages 69 to 74 ("Safety at Horse Shows"), loading and unloading a horse can be dangerous. Until you're confident and comfortable with the procedure, have a more experienced person load and unload your horse. Many horses object strenuously to shipping. It's far better to have a professional deal with this behavior until you have more experience.

Trailering your horse is probably the most dangerous part of show day for you and your horse. With commonsense precautions and good protection, shipping should go smoothly and safely.

CHAPTER FIVE

Tips for Your First Show

ALL SYSTEMS ARE GO. You're finally attending a horse show to ride, not to watch! There are several tips that can make the difference between a successful show and a disappointing experience. These tips range from advice on warming up, schooling, and ring savvy to evaluating your performance. Again, focusing on the fun aspects of showing can also make the difference between happiness and frustration.

The best attitude to have is one of eager acceptance, acknowledging that show results are unpredictable your first time out (and for a while after that, as well). If the only way you'll be happy is to get a blue ribbon, you're setting yourself up for disappointment. Don't set goals that are too lofty for your first show. The main objectives should be to have a safe, enjoyable time, and to learn something new.

There is no way on earth that you'll remember everything you should know at your first show. You're likely to forget many things, but don't fret or lose sleep over that fact. As you attend more shows, your way will become clearer and easier.

Many mistakes are made by riders at their first shows. My first was an open schooling show at a neighboring stable. I managed to find my diagonals, but I couldn't get my horse to canter on the correct lead. So although I didn't pin in my equitation canter class, I earned a second place in walk-trot equitation.

At my second horse show, the riders were asked to dismount and remount. I didn't check the snugness of the girth before remounting and I ended up under my horse's belly with the saddle, sitting in the mud in the pouring rain. I pinned sixth in a class of six. Fortunately, my parents encouraged me to use these experiences as learning tools and to move forward from there.

When showing, nothing ventured—nothing gained. No matter what happens, keep your chin up and maintain your sportsmanship. Above all, enjoy yourself.

Perhaps the most important tip you'll ever receive about showing is a deceptively simple one—breathe! Many riders in their first shows get so nervous they forget to breathe. It's common to see riders take one breath at the beginning of the class, and then take irregular gulps of air as they compete. I've even witnessed riders faint from lack of oxygen and fall off their horses!

There are several ways to learn to breathe effectively. Individuals who play a wind instrument or sing in a choir already know how to breathe with the diaphragm. The diaphragm is located just below your lungs. In order to breathe with your diaphragm, place one hand flat between your belly button and chest. Take a very deep breath— you should feel your hand rise over your diaphragm. Practice taking deep breaths using your diaphragm.

Deep, even, and regular breaths will allow your brain to get the oxygen it needs. Practice this style of breathing as you walk, trot, canter, and jump. Although it will seem forced at first, eventually it will be second nature.

Another method for achieving proper breathing is very simple— practice good posture. Sit up, spread your shoulder blades, and look ahead, not down. This position enables your lungs to work easily without constriction. Concentrate on breathing deeply and evenly. Practice this on horseback and while walking or sitting.

Some breathing problems are the result of physical conditions such as asthma or allergies. The excitement and stress of a horse show may make asthma and allergies worse. Horse shows are also full of allergens—dust, molds from hay, and even horses themselves can bring on allergy or asthma attacks. There are a number of medications that can ease your breathing and give peace of mind. Consult with your physician for the best method of coping with this problem.

The foundation for a good time starts at home even before you leave for the show. Let's start getting organized for a fun and relaxing show.

BEFORE YOU LEAVE HOME

Your show experience begins at home. The night before a show, organize your riding habit and equipment, pack the items that can be packed ahead of time, and then get a good night of sleep. Remember to pack any personal items you need such as eyeglasses and medications, as well as your checkbook. See the following pages for checklists.

Set out the clothes you'll wear to the show so you won't have to think about that in the morning. Most of us are a bit fuzzy upon arising for a show at four or five o'clock in the morning, so try to do as much as possible the night before. Set your alarm to ring early enough to have plenty of time to get dressed and ready.

Your mental warm-up can start the night before the horse show. In bed, relaxed and drifting off to sleep, picture yourself competing at the show. Imagine yourself riding well, enjoying the show, and getting a ribbon. Review your lessons in your mind and the goals you hope to accomplish. Many successful riders and athletes use this type of positive imaging to bolster their confidence.

Once you're awake, perform some simple stretches to limber your muscles. Mentally review again what you wish to accomplish over the course of the show. At breakfast, don't overeat or indulge in rich food—your stomach will thank you later. If your horse lives in your yard, make sure he gets an early breakfast so he doesn't have to be trailered on a full stomach. If he boards at a stable, arrange to have someone feed him early.

If you're particular about food, you may want to pack a lunch and snacks. Horse show food tends to be a bit unimaginative and even indigestible if you're nervous. The standard fare includes hot dogs, hamburgers, doughnuts, and soda, which cover the three basic food groups of fat, salt, and sugar. It would also be considerate to bring along lunch and snacks for your trainer and groom, if they're part of your team.

Checklist of What to Bring to the Show for You
- Riding jacket
- Ratcatcher
- Choker pin
- Gloves
- Riding boots
- Extra laces, if you have field boots (in case one breaks)
- Breeches or jodhpur pants
- Jodhpur straps
- Crop or bat
- Socks
- Belt
- Hairnet
- Hair clips or bobby pins
- A change of clothes
- Snacks and lunch
- Your favorite coffee cup
- Personal items—eyeglasses, medications
- Checkbook
- A sense of humor

Checklist of What to Bring to the Show for Your Horse
(Note: Some of the equipment on this list the horse will actually be wearing to the show.)
- Hoofpick
- Brushes
- Sponge
- Sweat scraper

- Mane comb
- Rub rags
- Fly spray
- Buckets
- Hay
- Grain (if needed)
- Bedding (if needed)
- Hay net
- Bridle
- Martingale (if needed and allowed)
- Saddle
- Girth
- Saddle pad
- Halter
- Lead line
- Lunge line (if needed)
- Lunge whip (if needed)
- Cooler
- Blankets or sheets, depending on the weather
- Shipping wraps
- Tail wrap
- Bell boots
- Head bumper
- Water (if it's not available on the grounds)
- First-aid kits: one for horses, one for humans
- A copy of your horse's negative Coggins test
- A copy of your horse's registration papers (if needed)
- A health certificate (if needed)
- Carrots or other horse treats

Last, remember to leave your dog at home. Dogs at horse shows are a nuisance and a hazard. If you feel guilty about leaving him home alone all day, make arrangements for a neighbor to take him for a walk.

Now let's head to the show grounds.

ARRIVING AT THE SHOW GROUNDS

Safely driving and parking your car or horse trailer is the first step when arriving at the show grounds. Always drive slowly through the grounds and parking area; many horses are easily spooked by cars. Never drive up directly behind a horse, and don't beep your horn anywhere on the grounds.

If you have a horse trailer, try to park well away from the show rings. It will be more restful and relaxing for both you and your horse. Many competitors like to park as close as possible to the show rings, secretary, and food, but I prefer not to. I enjoy having as much privacy as possible.

Check out the ground before you park; you don't want to get mired in mud with a loaded trailer. Always make sure that you can get out of your parking spot easily in case of emergency. When parking, be sure that there's as much room as possible between trailers so that riders and horses can walk safely through the area.

If you've driven your car to the grounds, park in the area designated for cars. Many shows have separate parking areas for cars and for horse trailers. Respect the wishes of the management and park where they suggest. Should all your required clothing and equipment be in your car, drop off what you need at the horse trailer, then go park.

Once you've unloaded your horse and car, find where the water is located. If it's a hot day, take care that both you and your horse don't get dehydrated. Some horses won't drink "strange" water, so it's always a good idea to bring along drinking water from home. You can use the show water to bathe your horse and cool him down.

Find out where all the show services, telephone, and food concessions are located. Visit the secretary's booth to sign in and pick up your number. Check for any changes in the schedule or location of your classes. If your pony needs to be measured to be eligible for a division, find out where the show steward has set up. Do you want a picture of you and your horse? See if there's an official show photographer.

Horse show secretary's booth at Fred's Farm in Chatham, New York.

Most larger shows have a farrier and veterinarian on the grounds, so seek them out if you require their assistance. Other shows generally have a farrier and veterinarian "on call." Don't hesitate to call them if you have a problem—that's why they're on call.

Check out where the emergency medical technician (EMT) or ambulance is located in case of emergency. If you have an unusual medical condition, let the EMT know in case you have a problem during the day. For example, I'm allergic to bee stings, so I always seek out the EMT and tell him.

The larger the show, the more services it will have. At large, A-rated shows, you'll often find tack shops, clothing, jewelry, art, and gifts on the grounds. There are people who go to these shows for shopping, not just riding! There's also usually a better food selection available at the big shows.

It's important to know where the bathrooms are. Invariably, you'll need to use the bathroom right before a class, so make sure you know where you're going. Many shows now put portable toilets right next to the show rings for the convenience of competitors.

Once you're situated and know your way around the grounds, it's time to warm up and school.

Warming Up and Schooling

A good warm-up and schooling session before your classes is essential for you and your horse. It helps you to loosen up both physically and mentally. This is also the time to deal with any last-minute problems or concerns you may have, such as stiffness of horse or rider, undue nerves, or broken equipment.

After arriving at the show, hand walk your horse around the grounds. This will familiarize both of you with the layout of the rings and the schooling area. It will also walk out any traveling "kinks" or stiffness your horse may have. As a beginner, there's a good chance your horse will have attended many more shows than you have. It's far better for you to begin showing with a horse or pony who knows the ropes. A horse who has never been to a show will be as nervous as you are—and that can be a poor combination.

While tacking your horse, double-check the leather for wear and safety. After tacking up, proceed to the designated schooling area. Don't ride or school in any other place, as there may be hidden hazards or inconsistent footing. Have your coach accompany you to warm-up. If you don't have a coach, ask a friend to come with you to offer suggestions. It's always a good idea to have someone accompany you for safety reasons. She'll be able to help you catch your horse if you fall off, and provide moral support.

Your goal in the schooling area should be to loosen up physically and mentally. This is just as important for your horse, who might be nervous too. Even old school horses

Catherine B. Knight

Last minute instructions before heading into the schooling area.

sometimes become flustered when brought to a show. A quiet warm-up in the schooling area helps most horses settle down. The exceptions are young, green horses, who generally need many shows to become seasoned. However, if you're a beginner show rider, you shouldn't be mounted on a young spitfire.

Use your time in the schooling area to work at each gait you'll perform. If you're jumping in a class, jump a few fences first in the schooling area. Make sure to school in both directions of the ring. Work enough that you feel comfortable and loosened up, but not so much that you're tired by the time your class starts. Remember, if you don't know something, you're not going to suddenly learn it at the show. Overschooling is just as bad as no warm-up at all.

Have your coach help you with last-minute pointers. Refine your position and work on correct pace. Ask any questions you think of, even if they sound silly. Observe your fellow competitors; if they're doing something you don't understand, ask your coach. Have your coach help you negotiate around other horses and riders if the ring is crowded.

Schooling areas at horse shows can look like bumper-to-bumper traffic on an expressway, complete with fender-benders. Riders coming and going, horses bucking, ponies whinnying, and coaches shouting—be prepared to ride defensively. Try to keep as much distance as possible between yourself and other riders.

If people are schooling over fences, be prepared to give the right-of-way to anyone who's on a jumping line. The term "heads up" is often used by riders to indicate their intentions. If you hear "heads up—outside line," it means the rider intends to jump the outside line of fences. Your response should be to politely get out of the way as quickly as possible.

Time permitting, it's better to get dressed in your show clothing after schooling, so your show clothing will be clean for your classes. An alternative is to wear overalls or a sweatsuit over your show clothing while you're schooling. The first time you get splattered by mud from a runaway pony, you'll understand why.

If your class is not about to start, get off your horse. Don't sit on your horse for more than ten or fifteen minutes while waiting for a class. Horses get tired and stressed out, too, and should not be used as an armchair for your convenience.

Now that you've signed in with the secretary, schooled, and warmed up, it's on to the show ring.

RING SAVVY—CATCHING THE JUDGE'S EYE

You can be the best rider in a class but you'll never receive a ribbon if you don't "show" yourself off. It's your responsibility to make sure the judge sees you, and sees you in the best light. There's a knack to knowing when to show off and when to hide.

Prior to your class, spend some time watching other classes. Observe how the judge officiates. Does she judge from inside or outside of the ring? Different judges have different preferences. Watch the judge and see how she tracks the riders around the ring. Does she turn around and follow the individual riders, or does she stay in one spot and judge? This information can be useful when it's your turn to show.

Does the judge seem to favor one style or position over another? Each judge has his or her pet peeves and favorite styles. Some judges emphasize leg position, others weigh posture or hand position more. Ascertain what the judge is looking for. Discuss with your coach how this will pertain to you.

Just before entering the ring, have a friend wipe your boots to remove the dust. Brush dirt and lint off your jacket if necessary. Double-check that your girth is snug. Give your horse a final brush or rub with a rag. Put your number on at the last minute so that it's "crisp" and not bent and worn. Little touches like these can make the difference in overall appearance and initial appeal to the judge.

Listen carefully to the announcer. When it's your turn to show, enter the ring promptly. If you're one of the first riders in the ring, use the time to do a quick warm-up. Trot or canter once around the ring to get a feel for it. Be aware that the judge might be watching even though the class hasn't started. First impressions really count! Don't chat with friends, ride sloppily, or visit over the fence with your family.

When the class is called to order by the judge or ringmaster, be ready. Usually the announcer or ringmaster will say, "Class is now in order" or "You are now being judged." Respond quickly and smoothly to the ringmaster's commands. Try to find an open space so that it will be easy for the judge to see you. Don't get trapped along the rail with riders blocking you from her vision. Should you find yourself in a traffic jam, circle across the ring and find an open space. If your show number is the type that's on a string and fastens around your waist, slide it over from the middle of your back to the side the judge is on. Remember to slide it to the other side when you reverse direction, and to the middle of your back for the lineup. This makes it easy for the judge to spot you; you never want her to have to struggle to see your number!

The winner of the class may not be the best rider, but the smartest one. You need to know how to present yourself to the best advantage. If you experience difficulty during the class—a wrong diagonal or lead, for example—try to hide it from the judge. Circle behind the judge's back until you've resolved the problem or purposely get lost in a crowd. When you're ready, emerge from the group and find an open space.

In large classes it's especially important to ensure that the judge

Brianna Gillies trotting in an equitation class finds an open space in the ring.

Catherine B. Knight

sees you. At least once at each gait make a pass directly in front of her. You may circle to get in front of the judge, but don't do it incessantly. Endless circling is annoying to the judge, and will have the opposite effect of what you intended.

When the ringmaster calls for you to reverse, look around to ensure that you won't bump into another rider when you turn. The best way for a beginner to reverse in an equitation or hunter class is using a simple half circle, sometimes called a simple reverse. You may also cut across the ring or walk across the diagonal of the ring. More advanced riders in an equitation class will reverse using a turn on the forehand or a turn on the haunches. Generally, a half circle to reverse is sufficient in most hunter and pleasure classes.

When it's time to line up, your horse should be standing square with his two front feet even and his back feet even or slightly apart. Check your position, sit up straight, and keep your heels down. Don't talk with the other competitors—you're still being judged! A judge will mark her card throughout the class to enable her to pick out who she feels are the winners. In very close classes, the lineup is when the judge makes her final decisions.

Once the judge's card has been handed in to the ringmaster or announcer, you may quietly compliment or congratulate other competitors. Give your horse a pat whether or not you receive a ribbon. Most shows announce ribbon winners in the order of first through sixth, but some go from sixth to first.

In over fences classes, competitors ride one at a time, so you'll be alone in the ring. However, you still want to make an impression on the judge. Unless you've received directions otherwise, always open and finish your round with a courtesy circle. A courtesy circle should be performed in front of your first fence and after your final fence. This allows the judge to evaluate your position or the horse's movement. It also ties the course together with a definite beginning and end. Remember to project a businesslike image the moment you step into the ring. You have just a few seconds to show your expertise, so be ready to shine!

HORSE SHOW RIBBON COLORS IN THE UNITED STATES*

Some other countries use a different color order. Many use a red ribbon for first place. Most shows in the United States award ribbons for placings from first to sixth.

first:	blue	sixth:	green
second:	red	seventh:	purple
third:	yellow	eighth:	brown
fourth:	white	ninth:	gray
fifth:	pink	tenth:	light blue

Champion:	blue, red, and yellow
Reserve Champion:	red, yellow, and white
Grand Champion:	blue, red, yellow, and white
Reserve to Grand Champion:	red, yellow, white, and pink

If something goes wrong while you're on course, try to make the best of it. Should your horse refuse a fence, circle back and try it again. If your horse refuses more than three times, politely leave when the judge excuses you from the ring. Refusals and disobedience are things you'll need to work on in the schooling ring or at lessons. If you fall off, catch your horse and either remount or lead the horse and leave the ring. Should you go "off course" (take the fences in the wrong order), excuse yourself from the ring. Under no circumstance should you harshly whip or punish the horse. And, in accordance with show etiquette, no matter what has gone wrong, you must ask the judge for permission to leave the ring.

When you receive a ribbon, nod (for women and girls) and/or tip your helmet (for boys seventeen and under) and thank the ringmaster and judge. Men should remove helmets when receiving a ribbon. (See page 63). On your way out of the ring, thank the gatekeeper for holding the gate open for you. If your trainer was ringside, express your gratitude for his support.

If you have more classes later in the day, try to keep clean. This is no easy task at a horse show. Change out of your show clothes or wear something over them if necessary. Depending on the amount of time to the next class, you may consider untacking your horse. Check to see whether he needs a drink of water or to be walked cool. If you're uncertain, ask for your trainer's opinion.

Now that the show is over, let's evaluate your performance.

Evaluating Your Show Performance

Are ribbons won the way to measure your performance? Absolutely not! You might not have done your best, but the competition was such that you won anyway. Conversely, your performance might have been flawless, but you didn't receive a ribbon. It can feel worse to get a ribbon you didn't deserve than to be overlooked for a fine performance.

The best way to evaluate your show performance is to examine whether or not you accomplished the goals you set for the show. (See pages 31-34, "Mental Preparation.") Were you able to incorporate everything you learned in lessons? Did you correct mistakes quickly and subtly? If you're unhappy with the way you rode, what could you have done differently? If you rode well and achieved your goals, what made the performance come together for you? How can you remember to repeat what you did well? Did you learn something new? And most important, did you have fun?

I know a woman who considers a show a success if she doesn't fall off her horse. She started riding at age forty-eight and isn't terribly athletic. However, she loves to ride and attend horse shows. She has a wonderful time whether or not she wins a ribbon. The joy of showing for her is in the simple act of participating. She's now in her sixties and her grandchildren consider her a hero. For that matter, everyone else thinks so too!

You may find that you place too much pressure on yourself to perform well. One good way to put all riding and showing into perspective is to attend a therapeutic horse show. North American Riding for the Handicapped Association (NARHA) has accredited programs and instructors all over the country. The children and adults entered in these shows have radically different goals from those of your average show rider. Although they enjoy winning ribbons, the victories for them are just in riding or driving a horse. Their courage is something we can all learn from.

The days after the show are a time to review the experience. Reflect, but do not dwell, on your performance. Don't beat yourself up over mistakes. Attempt to learn from your errors so you don't repeat them. Use your coach and riding instructor as a sounding board. Ask them to relate their best and worst beginner show experiences. You may find that

Courtesy of the American Morgan Horse Association

This 74-year old rider, Arlene Pizzi, is an inspiration to us all.

Participation in NARHA programs can be revitalizing for all riders.

(Photo courtesy of the North American Riding for the Handicapped Association, Inc.)

you're expecting too much out of yourself at this stage.

If you're unhappy with your performance at the show, take steps to improve the next time out. With your instructor, set up a lesson plan that will target your weak areas. Channel your disappointment into positive action. Establish new goals and a game plan to achieve them.

Sometimes a truly bad show experience is the best thing in the world for your riding. It makes you reevaluate your abilities and perhaps set different goals. Never, ever let a bad performance put an end to your dreams. Treat it as a momentary setback and focus your energies on improving in the future.

There are three main types of show personalities: perfectionists, pessimists, and optimists. Perfectionists are never happy with a performance because something always could be improved. Pessimists think their riding will never get better. Optimists usually have the most fun because they know everything, including their riding, will improve! Most of us have a combination of these traits. Strive to emphasize the optimist in your personality at horse shows and in life. It will open your mind to endless possibilities and enable you to attain your dreams. Optimists are better able to evaluate their showing realistically and take positive steps to improve themselves and their horses. They know that if they don't win, there's always another show.

FOCUSING ON FUN

I have friends, both amateurs and professionals, who perform in a show or two every week to amass points for year-end championships. This can become a repetitive grind, taking a lot of the joy out of showing. However, many of them have found great ways to release tension and have fun despite the serious nature of what they're doing. A conscious effort is made to "play" at horse shows. People joke, give pretend "awards" to fellow competitors, play pranks on one another, and help and encourage one another. They have developed a social system through the horse show circuit. This extended family arrangement even includes evening meals, transporting horses together, and sharing hotel rooms.

An example of a fun prize is the Ned Neat award. One rider's spouse has been nicknamed "Ned Neat" because of his fanatical organization and cleanliness at horse shows. He helps not only his wife and daughter, but also anyone else who needs assistance. Break a martingale? Ned Neat will run and get a new one for you. Your daughter is in tears because she did poorly? Ned Neat will console and encourage her. Riders on the circuit got together and presented him with a baseball cap emblazoned NED NEAT. Just seeing him in his cap on the showgrounds is enough to make everyone smile.

Pranks and jokes that are amusing, not cruel, can also keep things in perspective. I know of an amateur jumper rider who always complained that her horse was too big. She's about 5 feet tall, and her horse is about 17.1 hands. She constantly joked that she wished she could shrink her horse. Then, one day, when she went to get her horse out of his stall for class, she received a bit of a surprise. In the stall was a miniature horse the same color and with identical markings as her own horse.

Some shows offer costume or game classes. This helps lighten the mood and allows people to play. These are often scheduled during lunch to help break up the day. Many competitors take great joy in dressing their horses and themselves in ridiculous outfits. One unforgettable group dressed their horse as a camel, complete with two humps, and themselves as harem girls. Years later, they still get teased about this.

If you're starting to take things too seriously at shows, try something different. Last summer, I was feeling burned out and tired. Between judging and showing, it suddenly wasn't fun anymore. Friends cajoled me into showing something I had never attempted—Appaloosa Western Pleasure. Appaloosa Western Pleasure is judged on the horse's ability to be a good Western pleasure mount. The horse should be well mannered, obedient, and move evenly. Showdown's Shogun ("Gunnie") was kind enough to lug me around the ring. Can I ride well western? No. Did I have fun? You bet! I borrowed clothing from four people, and Gunnie and his tack from his owner, Dot Clark. Dot gave me a quick lesson, then it was off to the

Hallie McEvoy

Costume classes can be great fun.

Judith Wyman Strobridge

Author mounted on Showdown's Shogun.

ring. I started the class by praying I wouldn't fall and by the end of the class, I was relaxed, laughing, and having a wonderful time. We received a third in a large pointed class, and that ribbon means more to me than any other I've won in the past few years. Gunnie and the whole crew at the show gave me a priceless gift.

Trying something different doesn't have to shift far from your normal routine. If you only show in the hunter division, enter an equitation class for a change. Memorize a dressage test and enter a dressage show. Borrow a sidesaddle, take some lessons in it, enter all the regular classes that you normally would, and do the best you can. Try a games division. Volunteer at a therapeutic horse show. Vary your routine, and don't be afraid to be silly and joyful!

CHAPTER SIX

Purchasing a Show Horse or Pony

YOU HAVE NOW SHOWN for a few months and enjoy it, and want to continue with your riding and showing. Your mounts have been borrowed or leased horses and ponies. They've come from your riding academy or friends who've been kind enough to lend their horses to you. Although you've enjoyed your showing experiences, you feel held back without a permanent four-legged partner. It may be time to get your own horse.

Owning your own horse or pony has both advantages and drawbacks. The strong points include the joy of being able to ride and practice every day, building a partnership with your horse, and developing an emotional attachment to your equine friend. The drawbacks include the expense of boarding or keeping a horse, the time required to take care of a horse, and dealing with the inevitable emotional trials of ownership.

The biggest argument against owning your own horse is expense. Horses are expensive in every area—boarding, feeding, shoeing, veterinarian visits, tack, equipment, and the inevitable unexpected costs. However, at your level, the greatest gains in your riding and feel for horses will only be made with the partnership that comes with owning or leasing your own horse. And can a price be put on love?

There are several basic steps to follow in your quest to find the "ideal" show horse. First, establish a budget to avoid wiping out the family finances. Look at horses for sale, accompanied by your coach or riding instructor. Following that, "test ride" at least several horses. Consider the talents and disposition of each horse, along with the results of an examination by the veterinarian. Finally, after you've made your choice, you'll need tack that fits the horse and is comfortable for you.

Let's start on the path to becoming a horse owner.

WORKING WITH A TRAINER TO LOCATE A HORSE

There's a myth among beginner riders that there's a "perfect" horse just waiting for them. Unfortunately, there's no such thing as a perfect horse. Each one you try will have some drawback, no matter how small. It may be his conformation, attitude, size, age, perhaps his price. The art in purchasing a suitable horse is in deciding what your priorities are, and what problems you and your trainer can live with in a horse.

Expect to pay your trainer or riding instructor for her expert opinion. Most trainers are compensated in one of two ways: either with a daily "horse hunting" fee or with an agent's commission on the sale of the horse. This payment covers her expenses and time spent working on your behalf. The daily fee paid by the rider looking to buy the horse is especially important when a rider has her trainer run all over looking at horses, then elects not to purchase one. The manner in which the commission comes to pass is thus: The trainer finds a horse for sale, checks him out, decides if he's suitable for you, then arranges for you to try the horse. The seller of the horse pays your trainer a commission if you buy the horse. The standard commission is 10 percent of the price of the horse, unless otherwise specified by the seller.

Many people think there's a conflict of interest if the trainer has a stake in the sale of the horse. You could have your trainer help find you a horse by having her act as a buyer's agent. You'd be responsible for paying her either a flat "finder's fee" or a set amount when you purchase a horse. If you don't purchase a horse, you're still responsible for any expenses she has incurred during the search.

As you go about trying out horses, you'll find some horses who you'll love, but your trainer dislikes. Listen to your trainer! If she thinks an animal is unsuitable for you, no matter the reason, trust her judgment and expertise. Often a trainer can detect minute lameness or behavioral problems that you wouldn't see. Your experience as a beginner or intermediate is limited, and you may not make the wisest decisions. Listen to the voice of common sense from someone who's not emotionally involved.

When judging, I often see beginners mounted on inappropriate, unsafe, and even lame equines. In chatting with the riders and trainers it invariably comes out that the horse was bought against the trainer's advice. These are the most common reasons that unsuitable horses are bought by beginners:

1) "He was cheap."
2) "He was pretty."
3) "He was black (or white, or spotted, and so on)."
4) "He was young, and I want my child to grow up with her horse."
5) "He was old, so I thought he would be quiet and gentle."
6) "He came with tack, so I wouldn't have to buy any."
7) "I fell in love at first sight."
8) "I know my daughter can train him, even though she's only ten years old."

Unfortunately, some people feel they're experts after only a year or two of lessons, but selecting a horse without guidance after only a year or two of involvement with them is asking for trouble. A rider, or parents, might venture forth to buy a horse on their own, either in an attempt to save money by not taking the trainer along, or because they think they're capable of picking out a horse themselves.

The money that's saved by not getting a trainer's advice is deceptive. Should the horse require further training to be safe or pleasant, a lot of unnecessary money will be spent in this manner. If the horse is lame or has veterinary problems, further expense will be incurred to make the horse ridable. Either way, it would have been prudent to get an expert opinion from the start. The cost might be greater up front, but the long-term prospects are much better.

Here's a quick test to help determine if you're capable of picking out a horse that will be safe and suitable for you.

1) What is "founder" and what is its technical name?
2) What is the difference between an equitation class and a hunter class?
3) Name two types of grain horses eat.
4) Name the most common causes of colic.
5) What are degree pads? Where are they used?
6) How and under what circumstances should a standing martingale be used?
7) What is the height difference between a horse and a pony, and how is height in horses measured?
8) Name three types of hay.
9) How much and how often should a horse be fed?
10) What does the acronym AHSA stand for?

Answers:
1) In simple terms, founder is an inflammation of the sensitive laminae in the feet brought on by mismanagement, overfeeding, or stress. Laminitis is its technical name.
2) An equitation class is judged on the rider; a hunter class is judged on the horse.
3) Oats and corn.
4) Overfeeding, worms, lack of water, change of feed or hay, not properly cooling out a horse after exercise, extreme changes in weather, or change in residence.
5) Degree pads are commonly used on horses that have a navicular condition in their feet, or other lameness problems. The farrier will put them between the shoe and the hoof.

6) A standing martingale is a piece of tack that's used to keep a horse from raising his head too high. It's used for safety and control on high-headed horses. Standing martingales have two parts: One runs around the neck and the other is a strap between the nose band and the girth.

7) Horses are measured in "hands." An equine of over 14.2 hands qualifies as a horse. Any fully grown equine 14.2 hands and under is considered a pony. Four inches equals one hand.

8) Timothy, alfalfa, clover.

9) The amount of grain a horse is fed depends on several factors—his age, weight, metabolism, exercise level, and health. There's no firm answer. These factors also hold true for how many times a day a horse is fed. Most people feed their horses two or three times a day; some even feed four or five times a day.

10) American Horse Shows Association.

If you hesitated on even one answer, you're not ready to choose a horse on your own. It takes many years and much sweat to be a capable horseman. Consult with your trainer before purchasing any horse or pony. Even if you answered all the questions quickly and correctly, it's always a good idea to get a second opinion. It's especially important to get input from your trainer, as he's the one who'll be working with you and this animal.

FINDING AND TRYING HORSES AND PONIES

Where is the best place to find your future partner in showing? There are several good places to begin your search. The first is the stable at which you currently ride. Check with your instructor to see if your favorite lesson and show horses are for sale or lease. Occasionally, you may get lucky and your search will end there. But if not, next ask your instructor if she knows of any wonderful horses that are for sale at neighboring stables. These may be horses that your trainer has seen in the show ring. Ask someone who rides at that barn if he knows anything about these horses.

If neither method produces results, there are several other options. Scan the "Horses for Sale" classified ads in your local paper and regional horse publications. Have your trainer call and investigate any likely prospects. You'll need to learn the language to pick up warning signs of problems embedded in certain key phrases. Examples of these terms are "spirited" (translation: uncontrollable), "bomb proof" (translation: elderly and hard of hearing), "green broke" (translation: not broke enough for a beginner), "professionally shown" (translation: the owner couldn't ride him, so he had to hire a professional), and "pretty" (translation: good-looking but scatter-brained).

CLASSIFIEDS—For Sale

Cherry Garcia is for sale. Owner off to college. 15.3 3/4 h. bay TB mare. 9 yrs. Always in ribbons at A shows in equitation & sm. jr. htrs. Qualified Harrisburg, Devon & Medal Finals '95 & '96. Can be seen at Cap. Challenge & Hbg. Video avail. Serious inq. only. (PA)
8-16-3t

Shire/TB 2-yr.-old filly. Going very well under saddle and on trails. Quiet and willing. Pretty mover, $3500. Perch./QH 3-yr.-old filly. Doing crossrails and trails. Very quiet. $4500. Both are excellent field hunter prospects with no bad habits. GA.
8-16-4t

Seeking employment: 16.3 h. ch. TB g., 8 yrs. by Night Before Last o/o Royal Head mare, super mover, lovely carriage, easy to work around, farm raised. This intelligent gentleman needs a job; wants to be a dressage horse. Owner has no time. Sale or lease. (TN)
8-16-3t

Handsome 16.1 h., 12-yr. dk. br. TB g. H/j, event, 3rd level. No vices. V. kind. Safe & dependable. Great hunter pros. $12,000. PA.
1t

Dispersal of quality English lesson horses: Safe, sane, attractive TB/QH potential. Hunter/jumper/Pony Club. $1800-$3500. Rustic Man Farm, Vershire, VT.
8-16-2t

Lovely Trakehner mare, bay, 10-yr.-old, 15.3 h., very pretty mover. Excellent potential to move way ahead in dressage. Lots of talent. Winning at training level. An excellent lady's dressage prospect. $8000. VT.
8-16-2t

Hanoverian/TB cross mare, 6 yrs., 16.3 h., very attractive. Nice mover and jumper. Eligible pre-green. Priced to sell at $10,000. (VA)
8-16-2t

Reading classified ads is one way to look for horses for sale. (Reprinted by permission of The Chronicle of the Horse.)

There are also professional horse brokerage services that keep long lists of horses for sale all over the country. A drawback, though, is that the people who keep the lists often have little or no contact with the horses. Hence, they're unable to tell you anything other than what the seller has shared with them. However, they do offer sheer volumes of horses and ponies, and several will probably interest you. Ask your trainer to check out any possibilities. These services charge their customers in different ways. Some bill you for access to their list, others take a percentage of any sale from the seller.

If you have a computer and modem, the Internet

can be another place to search for horses. Several sites have sprung up on the World Wide Web that offer lists of horses for sale. Pictures may be included. You can learn more about each horse, either through the Internet or via telephone. Payment for these services varies, so carefully check out all the fine print.

Buying a show horse from a dealer is an option that should be pursued with eyes wide open. Horse dealers make their living strictly from buying and selling horses. As with any profession, a few bad dealers give everyone a bad name. All negotiations and transactions with a dealer should be clearly defined and in writing. Any guarantee that's offered should be put down in writing and signed by all parties to the sale. Never visit a dealer without your trainer accompanying you. And remember, if a horse sounds too good to be true, he probably is.

Many summer camps sell or lease their horses at the end of each season. Talk to individual campers to get more information about each of the horses; you'll probably learn more than you wanted to. Most camp horses are used to beginners, and have at least performed in camp horse shows. They've also put up with a lot of different riders, so they tend to be tractable and adjust well to different situations.

Leasing, with or without an option to buy, is a good way to get to know a horse. A regular lease generally runs anywhere from one month to one year. Lease fees range anywhere from free to a thousand dollars or more per month for a show horse. Remember, leasing usually doesn't include board or other services. You'll have to pay additional fees for boarding, riding lessons, farrier, and veterinarian.

Many stables offer a lease arrangement called "half leasing." This is generally done with stable-owned lesson horses. The monthly lease fee is usually about half the price of board. You're allowed to ride, and sometimes show, the horse when the stable isn't using him. This works well for people who are unable to ride or groom every day. The horse is still used and taken care of by the stable, but you have special access to him.

One of the benefits of leasing is that there's no long-term commitment. The experience can serve as a dress rehearsal for horse ownership. The main drawback is that you're investing your money and time in an animal you won't keep. The best of both worlds is leasing with an option to buy. The money paid toward the lease can then be applied to the purchase price of the horse.

When negotiating to buy a horse or pony, try to get the seller to agree to a trial period, usually two weeks or less. A trial period is useful if you're unsure of the horse's personality or of your ability to ride him correctly. Not every seller will agree to a trial period, as many things can happen during the trial that could ruin the horse. Sellers are more likely to agree to a trial if the horse will be stabled in a good public barn under the supervision of a respected professional.

Both you and your trainer should test ride the horse. Observe your trainer riding the horse. Does the horse possess good manners? Is he willing? Is he a good mover? When you ride him, ask yourself these questions: Is he comfortable? Do you feel safe? Can you properly control him? Ask your trainer her opinion of your appearance on the horse. Are the two of you well matched in size? Do you look "nice" on the horse?

Find out why the horse is being sold. With horses and ponies that are suitable for beginner show riders, it's common that a horse will be outgrown within two or three years. There are very few horses that can take their riders from absolute beginners in the show ring to the National Horse Show. Don't expect a horse to be able to do every level with every person who rides him. A horse should be bought with just one main job description in mind for him—to be a safe, consistent, talented, and willing partner for you at this stage, and one level above, in your riding.

Find out how long the horse has shown. Although it's nice to know how many ribbons a horse has won, this is not necessarily a barometer of future performance in the show ring. Ask who rode the horse and received the ribbons. If the horse has been shown consistently by a professional rider, he may not have the same performance with you. Conversely, if you're a better rider than the former exhibitor, you may obtain better results.

Once you've found a horse that you enjoy, is priced within your budget, and meets your trainer's approval, it's time to call the veterinarian. You may have the veterinarian examine the horse before you make an offer, or else make a clean bill of health a contingency of the sale. When your offer has been accepted, expect to leave a deposit with the seller. Just saying you'll buy the horse is not enough. A deposit is required to hold the horse until the veterinarian checks him out or you take him home.

The transaction is a business one and you must act accordingly. Always get everything in writing when buying a horse. The bill of sale should list the horse's age, color, height, tattoo number (if he has one), general description, and sale price. If the sale is contingent upon any other factor such as veterinarian approval, list that as well. It's better to list more information than you think you need, in case of questions or problems later on. This information is also important if you plan to insure your horse for mortality or liability.

Most important, take your time looking for a horse. It's worthwhile to be thoroughly prepared; don't rush into the unknown. Although it may seem like you'll never find the right horse, suddenly one will appear. Your patience will pay off.

CONSULTING THE VETERINARIAN

Consulting the veterinarian is the most important step in purchasing a horse or pony. A thorough health examination may include X-rays, blood work, scoping to check breathing and wind, and a hands-on check of the hooves, legs, teeth, cardiovascular system, eyes, other senses, and reproductive system.

How much the veterinarian needs to check depends on several factors. The price to be paid for the horse has a bearing on how much work the veterinarian should put into it. An inexpensive horse being purchased for light and nonstrenuous riding probably doesn't need full X-rays and blood work, but should have a basic examination. Many "inexpensive" horses have turned into costly horses due to unexpected veterinary problems that would have been detected with a basic examination.

An expensive competition horse that will perform strenuous

work should have a complete and thorough examination. Many people want to skip this step because they're spending a lot of money on the horse, and are reluctant to spend more. This is a misguided attempt at saving, because if the horse has problems, you'll spend a lot more later on. An examination by a veterinarian will run

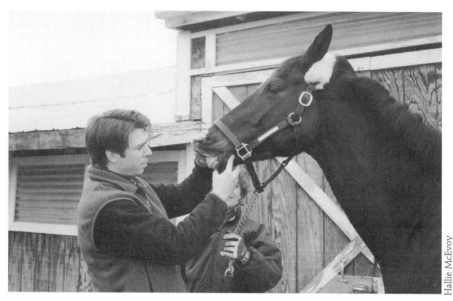

Hallie McEvoy

Dr. Kevin Landau, DVM, checks the teeth of Pavarotti as part of an examination.

from $75 to $350, depending on whether X-rays and intensive work are part of the checkup.

A horse to be insured for mortality will probably be required to have a full exam by the insurance company. Sometimes the insurance company will require a second opinion before it will insure him, especially if anything questionable arises during the exam. Check with your insurance agent for the necessary steps to take before calling the veterinarian.

Even if you're buying a horse you know well, and you think you know the complete background of the horse, it's still a good idea to have a veterinarian look him over. This is especially important for an older horse. Although a horse may look fit, he can have grave health and lameness problems that are not immediately noticeable to the untrained eye.

Hallie McEvoy

Farrier Scott Johansen fits a shoe to a hoof.

Consult with your farrier prior to any purchase. A horse is only as good as his feet. Some horses require extensive and expensive corrective shoeing to keep them sound; if that's the case, it can double or triple the standard farrier charges.

What should you do if a horse you want doesn't pass veterinary muster? There are several options. You can take the horse anyway and live with the problems uncovered in the veterinarian's examination. You can make a lower offer for the horse in keeping with his current health and soundness. You can pass on the horse entirely, and try to find another horse. What you do depends on the problems the horse has, your trainer's opinion, the veterinarian's advice, and your ability to cope with the horse's health problems.

Sometimes a horse will be deemed "serviceably sound" by the vet. Serviceably sound is a term that can have different meanings. It can mean a horse with an old "bow" (bowed tendon) who will stay sound with proper conditioning and preventive treatment, or a horse with impaired breathing because of heaves or allergies who will stay sound with medication.

The decision to purchase a horse who's serviceably sound should also be carefully considered. Listen carefully to your trainer, veterinarian, and farrier. Your family or spouse should also be consulted if the health or soundness problem will require extra time, effort, and expense on your behalf. All angles should be weighed to prevent heartache and financial distress later on.

There are many horses for sale. It's not necessary to settle for one that's unsound. Although you may have fallen in love with an unsound horse, he probably will break your heart. Unsound horses eat just as much as healthy horses, and cost the same to keep. It's better in the long run to purchase a sound and healthy horse who will be your companion in the show ring, on trails, and in the barn.

TALENT AND DISPOSITION OF DIFFERENT BREEDS

What horse and pony breeds are most suitable for beginners at hunter and jumper shows? There's no simple answer, but there are generalizations (with exceptions) in every breed. The best horse for showing is one that you enjoy riding, is safe, is sound enough to do the job, and allows room for you to grow and improve.

The best beginner show horse may be one of indeterminate origins. These "grade" horses can be observed at every show. They're usually plain or even homely, with big heads and swaybacks. Their conformation is often poor, and they lack the glamour of "breedier," showier horses. Look into their eyes and you'll see a docile, capable, willing spirit with a big heart. Very often, these are the horses that have the most ardent fans and are thought of as beautiful despite their shape. A common expression is "handsome is as handsome does." These are the horses that serve as the backbone and building blocks of the show industry. Horsemen refer to them as "packers," "saints," and "good eggs." They'll tolerate poor riders and long hours in the ring without complaint. Although the package might be plain, what lies inside these animals is pure gold. As Antoine de Saint-Exupéry said in *The Little Prince*, "It is only with the heart that one can see rightly; what is essential is invisible to the eye."

Thoroughbreds
At large, A-rated AHSA horse shows, the most common breed is the *Thoroughbred*. Thoroughbreds tend to be talented and athletic ("good movers") and good jumpers. They have the ability and fire that are required to succeed in hunters, jumpers, and equitation. Thoroughbreds tend to be a bit "hot," or high-strung, so they are not always the most suitable mount for beginners. However, as I mentioned above, there are exceptions within every breed. I see many Thoroughbreds safely and happily carrying beginners in small horse shows.

Thoroughbreds tend to be very athletic. Peter Townsend jumping Taylor Forbes.

Quarter Horses aim to please. (Photo by Watt McSadden, courtesy of the AQHA.)

Quarter Horses

Quarter Horses tend to make wonderful beginner mounts. Overall, they're quieter and more settled than Thoroughbreds. They usually don't have the same "step" and length of stride as a Thoroughbred, but make up for it in temperament. Many people prefer *Appendix Quarter Horses,* which have some Thoroughbred blood. This style of Quarter Horse gives the best of both worlds. Quarter Horses possess good, steady personalities and are thought of as "people pleasers."

The Color Breeds

Appaloosas, Pintos, Paints, Buckskins, and other *color breeds* can make fine hunter and jumper show horses. However, there's still some prejudice in many parts of the country against these breeds because they haven't traditionally been hunters and jumpers. You must examine whether you have a tough shell to withstand the occasional ignorant ribbing. There are currently a couple of great Appaloosas showing at nationally ranked shows that are changing people's opinions. I've seen many fine brightly colored horses carrying beginner riders safely and well.

Catherine B. Knight

Elizabeth Gollobin and Patti's Rerun, a buckskin, enjoyed their show.

Dawn Hough, aboard Litchfield Dixie Lee, a Morgan trained by Linda E. Smith, qualified for the Marshal Sterling Adult Jumpers (over 4 feet!) at the Washington International Horse Show.

(Courtesy of the American Morgan Horse Association)

Pennington Galleries

Morgans

The versatile *Morgan* breed is a good choice for a beginner. *Lippitt Morgans,* which can most closely be traced back to the founding sire, Justin Morgan, are particularly levelheaded. Morgans make fine trail as well as show horses. They tend to be wonderful family horses, as they can adapt to different riders and situations. Morgans are also a good driving horse, and will happily switch back and forth between riding and driving.

The Warmbloods

Various warmblood breeds are being seen more and more often in the show ring. *Trakehners, Hanoverians, Dutch Warmbloods, Swedish Warmbloods, Friesians,* and other warmbloods can be fine beginner's mounts, especially for adults. Warmbloods may have stubborn streaks, but are talented movers and jumpers. They tend to be on the tall side with large bodies, so they aren't suitable for small children or petite adults.

Draft Horses

Percheron, Cleveland Bay, and *Clydesdale* crosses are becoming increasingly popular. A common Percheron cross is with a

Hallie McEvoy

Wesseline, a champion Friesian mare.

Thoroughbred, often referred to as a "Thercheron." The draft blood of the Percheron combined with the Thoroughbred makes a good-moving, pleasant horse. They tend to be on the large side, however, so they're more suitable for tall teenagers and adults.

Arabians

Some *Arabians* make fine hunter and equitation horses for the lower levels of showing. They tend to be small and refined, so they are perfect for a growing child or small adult. Although many have the scope and ability, few Arabians are seen at the large hunter and jumper shows, as riders and trainers have been slow to accept them. However, for a beginner rider at smaller shows they can be the perfect mount. *Anglo-Arabians* have both Arabian and Thoroughbred blood, and are a very nice cross for showing.

Pony Breeds

There are several breeds that make fine show ponies. *Welsh ponies* are especially noteworthy. They're refined, attractive, and talented under saddle and over fences. They range in size from small to large pony height (small ponies are 12.2 hands and under; medium ponies

Catherine B. Knight

Christiana Knight cantering D'Artagnan, an Arabian.

are over 12.2 and up to 13.2 hands; and large ponies are over 13.2 and up to 14.2 hands.) Welsh ponies also tend to be incredibly smart and learn their lessons quickly.

Connemara ponies, although generally classed as a pony, can range up to 15-plus hands. These ponies are wonderful jumpers and are versatile, too. They're often seen pulling carts or foxhunting. Connemaras are a most suitable beginner mount for either a child or an adult. I knew a Connemara who took his owner from beginner shows all the way to the ASPCA Maclay National Equitation Finals—a remarkable feat!

Shetland ponies tend to be small or medium sized. One of the most popular beginner mounts for young children, they're round bodied with delicate faces, and are very intelligent. Shetlands are usually the escape artists of the barn—their prehensile lips can open doors, latches, and feed bins. They may display bratty pony behavior when they think they can get away with it.

Mules

In some parts of the country, it's perfectly acceptable to show a *mule.*

Rocky, a Welsh pony, is good to his riders.

Catherine B. Knight

This Connemara is a nice hunter.

(Photo courtesy of the American Connemara Pony Society)

Mules are half horse and half donkey—their dam (mother) is a horse and their sire (father) is a donkey. Mules that are half Thoroughbred can be wonderful jumpers with great temperaments, and are tolerant of a beginner's mistakes. Although mules are not allowed to show at AHSA-recognized shows, many schooling and open shows permit them, as do some dressage shows.

If you absolutely, positively, have to own a certain breed, contact the national or regional breed organization for more information. (See the list of clubs and organizations in the back of this book.) Make sure your trainer is comfortable with your breed choice. Most trainers are more concerned with how a horse performs than with his pedigree.

Meredith Hodges on Lucky Three Mae Bea C.T., was 1990 Mule Jumping World Champion.

Pro Photo, Pam Olsen

No matter what breed or type you choose, a beginner hunter seat show horse should possess most of the following characteristics. He must be:

1) safe
2) serviceably sound
3) an adequate mover
4) able to jump cross-rails or small fences with ease
5) tolerant of his rider's beginner mistakes
6) of pleasant temperament and well mannered
7) well broke with some show experience
8) easy to tack up, groom, and work around for the beginner

He does not necessarily have to be:

1) young
2) beautiful
3) 100 percent sound
4) bay colored
5) a great mover
6) expensive

As a beginner, the most suitable horse for you is one who is safe, quiet, forgiving, pleasant, and has some show experience. Do not rule any horse out because of his appearance, color, or breeding. Whether he's a Pinto or an Anglo-Arab, if he works for you, he's the one.

PRICE RANGES FOR BEGINNER
SHOW HORSES AND PONIES

An old joke that's told to prospective horse buyers goes this way:

Customer: "What does a show horse cost?"
Horse dealer: "How much do you want to spend?"

Another joke that hits home is:

Question: "How do you make a small fortune in the horse business?"
Answer: "You start with a big fortune."

Expect to pay anywhere between nothing and $50,000 (yes, $50,000) for a show horse or pony suitable for beginners. Realistically, the average price range is from $1,500 to $25,000. You probably are now clutching your chest and saying, "$25,000 for a pony?!?!" However, show horses and ponies routinely sell for prices in that range. Many people who'd never dream of spending $25,000 for a car are willing to spend that for a pony or a horse.

How much you spend for a show horse depends on several important factors. These include what you expect the horse to do, your riding ability, your trainer's expectations, and your pocketbook. The most important consideration in buying a horse is the safety factor. A horse can have everything else going for him, but if he's unsafe for you to ride, he's worthless. There is no price that can be put on safety.

A beginner show rider's needs from a horse are basic. He should be able to walk, trot, and canter both directions of the ring in a balanced, comfortable frame. He must be able to jump a low course of fences or cross-rails in a safe and pleasant manner. The horse must

These experienced ponies have much to teach their young riders.

also be forgiving of any mistakes that a beginner rider is bound to make. This horse need not be handsome or young. Often the most appropriate horses and ponies are a bit older (over the age of twelve) and are not beauty queens.

Depending on the region of the country in which you live, this "typical" beginner show horse or pony will cost between $2,500 and $7,500. At this price you should be able to get a horse that will be appropriate for your current level, and will also be able to take you one or two levels higher. Depending on the person, the transition from beginner to intermediate show rider can take anywhere from one to four years.

It's unrealistic to expect the same horse or pony to carry you from rock-bottom beginner classes all the way to the National Horse Show, especially if you've spent only $2,500. It has been done, but it's rare. A horse or pony that has the scope and ability to compete at a national level is rarely sold as a beginner's mount. These animals have a much bigger price tag.

A talented, healthy, "fancy" (very pretty and with excellent conformation and pedigree) young horse suitable for 1st Year Green Hunter classes (hunter classes over fences of 3'6 ") on a national level will often cost $25,000 to $250,000. These prices are clearly out of the range of most people who are just getting into the sport.

Sometimes you can find a horse suitable for showing for free. Occasionally, someone will want to find a good home for his retiring show horse. The horse may be older and unable to compete at the upper levels due to the routine stresses and strains of competition. However, he might be perfect for light showing as a beginner's mount. I know a little girl who's learning to show on a horse who competed successfully on multiple occasions at the National Horse Show. The horse is sound for beginner shows, but unable to keep up with the demands of the top shows. The horse was given to her with the provision that he never show over fences higher than 2 feet, or go to more than six shows a season. What a lucky little girl! This horse is teaching her the ropes of showing.

To find a free show horse, check with your trainer, local stables, and newspaper classified ads. Word of mouth can be an effective tool in locating a horse or pony. Often, a person giving away a horse will have a number of applicants. You need to demonstrate that you'll provide the horse with a secure and loving home. The person giving the horse away will also probably have some conditions on your use of the horse. These conditions might include stabling arrangements, training, level of showing allowed, and vitamins and supplements required.

When searching for horses to buy, establish a budget and stick to it. This budget must include related expenses such as veterinarian examination, farrier consultation, trainer's fees for time and expenses in horse hunting, commissions, and purchase of tack. If you have $5,000 to spend, you'd be wise to look at horses priced in the $3,500 to $4,000 range, so you won't overspend your budget.

Occasionally a seller will be willing to take payments over time. This is similar to making payments on a car or a new kitchen. A deposit is required up front, then the balance is paid off over a specified time. Be careful when considering this option. Often people spend more than they can afford because the monthly payments make it seem so easy. Caution must be applied to any financial dealing that will stretch the budget.

Do not consider a horse an investment. Unless you're wealthy and can afford to take huge risks with your money, a horse is never a "good" investment. Horses get sick, go lame, become injured, and even die. Horses are fragile animals despite their size and strength. Many horse ailments (such as colic) and accidents may necessitate euthanasia. These same illnesses might be considered minor problems in a dog or a cat. I've known a few horses who seemed suicidal in their quest to hurt themselves. When you purchase a horse, you must consider that you may never get your money back out of the horse. The value of the horse is in companionship, fun, and showing. Very few horses appreciate in actual monetary value.

If you're on a limited horse-buying budget, you must examine your options sensibly. You can't expect to buy a young, handsome, talented, sane, safe, and experienced show horse for $1,500. You might be able to buy a horse for $1,500 that has most of your requirements, and be happy with that. When you have a limited amount to spend, you need to be flexible in your desires and requirements. The qualities that you must never set aside, however, are safety and sanity. If you must compromise, looks, youth, and prior experience can be sacrificed.

Remember that after buying the horse, you still must have enough money to support him. Many people go all out on the purchase price of a horse, then struggle with the monthly maintenance payments. Only buy what you can safely afford and support. Plan your budget wisely and you'll enjoy your riding a lot more. Sound planning enables you to enjoy your horse without worrying unduly about finances. Consult with your trainer and other experts before making the plunge and buying a horse or pony.

PURCHASING TACK, EQUIPMENT, AND SUPPLIES

Unless you were lucky enough to buy a horse that came with well-maintained tack, you'll need to purchase it. Required tack and equipment include: *saddle, girth, bridle with bit, halter, blankets, sheets, coolers,* and *grooming supplies.* Many horses also need vitamins and daily supplements that are not usually included in board payments.

Monthly Maintenance Expenses of Horses

c   Board at a stable. This includes feed, hay, shavings, pasture, and labor.

c   Horses kept at home will require feed, hay, shavings, pasture, a stall, feed and water buckets, and storage space for all the supplies, as well as your labor.

c   Veterinarian.

c   Farrier.

c   Feed supplements and vitamins (usually not included in board).

c   Medications (if required).

c   Saddle, bridle, halter, and other tack.

c   Grooming supplies.

You must make a budget for buying tack and equipment. It's all too easy to walk into a tack store and overspend when you see all the nifty horse items. Surely your new horse needs that striped, all-wool custom cooler with matching wraps. And how about those pretend reindeer antlers for the barn Christmas party? (I hate to admit it, but my horse has a pair.) Curb those impulses.

Temptation surrounds you in a tack shop. Decide what you need before you go in. Make a list with the help of your trainer. Once you enter the store, don't purchase anything that's not on the list. Avert your eyes from equipment you don't need. Bring along your trainer or a friend to help you make wise decisions.

Without overspending, do buy the best tack and equipment you can afford. In the long run it's less expensive to purchase quality tack that will last than to replace inferior pieces every year. A saddle or blanket is not a bargain if it falls apart.

Used tack is an affordable option. Many tack shops have a section of used equipment. A good, nicely broken in used saddle is a wonderful alternative to a more expensive new saddle. When buying used equipment, make sure that the leather is in good condition with no cracks or dry rot. Saddles should be checked to make sure

A well-stocked tack shop.

the tree isn't broken. And any tack should fit both you and your horse properly.

If you bought a horse that came with tack, have your trainer look over the equipment to see that it's suitable and safe. A saddle or bridle may fit the horse but not be right for you. In this case, sell the equipment and put the money toward new or used tack that's more appropriate.

Saddles, Saddle Pads, and Girths

Any equipment made of leather needs to be closely examined. Leather manufactured in England, Germany, Switzerland, France, and the United States tends to be of better quality and is more expensive than leather from other countries. In general, leather produced in Hungary, Mexico, India, and Pakistan is inferior. The quality of leather from Argentina has improved dramatically in the past several years. Many fine saddles and bridles are now made there.

Expect to pay anywhere from $250 to $5,000 for a new leather saddle. The price for a good basic hunter seat show saddle is in the $450 to $1200 range. For around $1,000, you can purchase a fine, English-made saddle that will be comfortable for you and the horse, and last for years.

The type of saddle you buy will depend on your riding interests and your trainer's input. Most hunter seat show riders use a close contact or close contact with knee roll saddle. Some riders prefer an all-purpose saddle, which can be used for basic dressage as well as jumping. Specialized dressage saddles are awkward to use for jumping, and should only be purchased for dressage and flat work.

An alternative to leather has surfaced in the past few years. Synthetic saddles, made of nylon and other artificial fabrics, offer an affordable option—a brand new one will cost between $150 and $450. A drawback is that many people think they don't offer the same fit or "feel" as a leather saddle. Another problem is that there's still some prejudice against synthetic tack in the show ring. If you plan to show seriously, you should probably invest in a leather saddle.

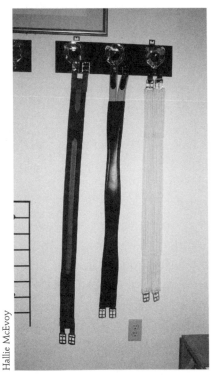

Hallie McEvoy

Three different types of girths. Left to right: nylon or "cloth" girth, shaped leather with elastic end girth, and a string girth.

Saddle pads protect the horse's back from rubs and protect the saddle from sweat. White fleece is the most appropriate for showing. As it's hard to keep a white, fluffy saddle pad clean around a horse, many people have an extra pad to use for schooling. Schooling pads can be any color you like—there are some wild combinations on the market. Saddle pads cost from $15 to $125. A nice show pad can be bought for about $30.

Girths now come in different materials including leather, cotton, and nylon, and in many styles such as folded, string, shaped, and with elastic stretch ends. Girths range in price from $20 for a string girth to $120 for one made of fine leather.

Bridles

Leather bridles suitable for lessons and showing will cost between $50 and $200. Bridles made of synthetic materials are available, but are generally frowned upon for showing. However, they're great for schooling and lessons. They also are weather resistant, so you never have to worry about getting stuck in the rain.

Bridles come in three sizes: pony, cob, and horse. Some companies are now making extra-large bridles to fit the influx of warmblood horses into the sport. In addition, bits come in many sizes and styles. Don't buy a bit without knowing what your horse will ride best in. Bits cost between $12 and $50.

Never buy a saddle or bridle before you buy the horse. The saddle may fit you, but it might not fit the horse. Saddles come in various seat sizes for the rider and tree widths for the horse. A poor-fitting saddle will make a horse miserable. Many tack shops and saddle companies will let you take home a saddle and try it on your horse. Have your trainer check the fit for both you and the horse.

Martingales

Some horses require a martingale. A martingale is a piece of equipment that helps keep a horse's head down within a certain frame. There are two types of martingales, *standing* and *running.* A standing martingale, commonly used for equitation and hunter classes over fences, runs from the girth and around the neck to the nose band. A running martingale, frequently used in jumper classes, runs from the girth around the neck to the reins. Many high-headed horses and ponies need a martingale for safety reasons. Martingales cost from $25 to $150.

Halters

The most basic piece of equipment is a halter for your horse. Halters come in either leather or nylon and cost from $10 to $125. Although nylon halters are colorful, many horsemen feel they're not safe. If a horse gets a nylon halter stuck on something, it won't break if he struggles to free himself. This can be dangerous. If you do buy a nylon halter, make sure it has a leather breakaway strap or another quick-release mechanism.

A standing martingale will discourage a horse from raising his head too high.

Catherine B. Knight

Supplies for Cleaning Tack

For all your leather equipment, you'll need conditioning supplies. Saddle soap and neatsfoot oil are used to keep your tack soft, supple, and well preserved. Any saddle will be ruined without proper care. All leather should be wiped down after every use to remove dirt, debris, and sweat. Bars of saddle soap cost $1 or $2. The price of neatsfoot oil varies from $4 for a small bottle to $25 for a year's supply.

Blankets, Sheets, and Coolers

Your horse will need a blanket and a sheet. Blankets cost from $35 to $300. Some are weather- and waterproof, allowing you to turn out your horse on wet-weather days. Sheets, which cost between $30 and $150, depending on the quality and durability, are of a much lighter weight than blankets, and are not designed to provide as much warmth and protection.

Coolers are used to cool down a horse after exercise. They come in a variety of fabrics including wool, cotton, and polyester blends. Some coolers are of mesh—they look like fishing nets. Expect to pay $35 to $200 for a cooler. Some shows award coolers as championship prizes. It's always nice to win one. (They make great blankets for your guest room, too.)

Grooming Supplies

You'll need a hard brush, soft brush, curry comb, mane comb, rub rag, and hoofpick. You should be able to pick up all these items for a total of about $25. Horse shampoos sell for $5 to $30, depending on the size of the bottle. Fly spray, coat conditioners, and other topical applications are a must to keep your horse happy. Basic first-aid supplies, such as lotions and disinfectants for cuts and scrapes, should also be purchased. A rectal thermometer is necessary to keep in case of illness, so you can take your horse's temperature.

Leg Wraps

Every horse should have at least one set of standing wraps and quilts. These are used for protection when shipping and for supporting injured legs. A set of four wraps will cost from about $8 to $20. A set of four quilts runs about $15. It's also helpful to have a set of four polo wraps. Polo wraps, used for support and protection while exercising, cost between $15 and $30.

Basic bathing and grooming supplies including several styles of brushes, mane comb, "Grooma" style curry comb, Show Sheen, sweat scraper, hoof pick and brush, bucket, half-moon sweat scraper, two types of shampoo, natural sponge, and a curry comb.

Tack Trunks

Once you've purchased all your equipment, you'll need a tack trunk to keep it all in. Tack shops sell trunks made of wood or plastic. Prices range from $50 up to $600 for a custom-designed trunk. You might purchase a large tool chest at the hardware or department store instead. These tend to be priced a little more reasonably. Another good storage option is an old "steamer" or "camp" trunk. Army/navy stores and camp supply stores stock them.

Nutritional Supplements

Nutritional supplements can be purchased at the feed store, veterinarian's office, or tack shop. The price depends on the ingredients. Most horses do well on a basic vitamin or supplement mix. Horses or ponies with special needs might require a stronger or more complex supplement. Health conditions such as weak hoof walls, the tendency to tie up (azoturia), and a poor coat can be dramatically improved with the correct vitamins and supplements. Consult with your veterinarian to determine what your horse will need.

Make sure that the stable manager understands the correct dosage of supplement for your horse. Write instructions on a 3 by 5 index card and place the card on the stall door. In many stables, every horse is on a different supplement, and it can get confusing for those whose job it is to feed them. It's also important to place a card on your horse's stall with your name, telephone number in case of emergency, as well as the name and number of the veterinarian you use.

A mineral or salt block should be available for your horse in his stall. Mineral blocks are a dull rust color, while salt blocks are white. Salt and mineral blocks are especially important for your horse during periods of hard exercise and in warm months. Check with your veterinarian for advice on which type of block to use. Small, stall-sized salt and mineral blocks cost $1 to $3. Wall holders for them cost between $2 and $6. Salt and mineral blocks can also be purchased in large, pasture-sized blocks to be shared among a herd of horses.

Your horse will need to be wormed every four to six weeks. There are several types of wormer on the market. Paste and powder wormers each destroy a different type of infestation. Paste wormers come in a "syringe" and are administered to the horse's mouth. Powder wormers may be added to the horse's feed. Many veterinarians recommend rotating wormers from month to month. This prevents worms from developing an immunity to the treatment. Additionally, some wormers are more effective at certain times of the year. Consult your veterinarian for the best worming program. Paste wormers cost between $8 and $15. There are also more expensive wormers on the market that can be added daily to your horse's feed. These wormers target only certain types of worms, however, so you'll still need to treat the horse for other worms from time to time.

Buying equipment and supplies for your first horse can be a budget challenge, but have fun with it. I enjoy shopping for my horse a lot more than for myself. She's also probably better dressed than I am—at least her clothes match! Remember the key points when going to purchase equipment: Make a list, bring a friend or your trainer, and consult with your veterinarian. With these in mind, your purchases will be sensible and essential.

Conclusion

MOST PROFESSIONAL HORSEMEN are involved with horses for love, not money. After all, there are far easier ways to earn a living than working twelve hours a day, seven days a week. Most horses and ponies I know are pampered pets, beloved members of their human families. It's common to see retired lesson and show horses grazing in the pastures of active stables. These horses haven't done anything for years, but they've earned their rest and a happy retirement. They don't "earn their keep," but they've given their lives to their riders, so they're treated as honored pensioners. Many horsemen do this at great hardship to their business, but some things are more important than the dollar.

I love horse shows, and feel honored to be part of the horse community. Being a judge for the American Horse Shows Association is a privilege and a joy for me. I strive every day to uphold the ideals of the talented horsemen who came before me, and I try to pass something on to the coming generations.

There are several rules that keep me focused and happy in riding and showing. They are:

- Be kind and humane to all animals and people.
- Learn something new about horses every day.
- Share the joy and knowledge of horses with everyone.
- Have fun as often as possible.
- Don't take yourself too seriously.

  c   Kiss pony muzzles frequently.

  c   Help feed the barn cats and get them spayed and neutered.

For riding instructors and trainers, I hope this book helps you remember what it was like to be a beginner. For parents and spouses of riders, may this book bring you greater understanding of the sport, and therefore of your loved ones. And especially, for new riders, I hope that this book inspires you to begin showing. Ride hard, play fair, and above all, have fun!

Two riders at the end of the day.

Appendixes

ORGANIZATIONS AND CLUBS FOR HUNTER SEAT RIDERS

The following list is designed to help you locate riding, showing, and breed organizations that have significance to you as a hunter seat rider. It isn't a complete list of every horse organization in the United States; contact your state horse council, the American Horse Council, and the American Horse Shows Association for additional organizations in your region or state.

Alaska State Horsemen
P.O. Box 141886
Anchorage, AK 99514-1886
(907) 346-1452

American Association of
  Horsemanship Safety
P.O. Drawer 39
Fentress, TX 78622-0039
(512) 488-2128

American Bashkir Curly Registry
P.O. Box 246
Ely, NV 89301-0246
(702) 289-4999

American Connemara Pony Society
2630 Hunting Ridge Road
Winchester, VA 22603
(540) 662-5953

American Donkey and Mule
  Association
2901 North Elm Street
Denton, TX 76201-7631
(817) 382-6845

American Grandprix Association
3104 Cherry Palm Drive,
  Suite 220
Tampa, FL 33619
(813) 623-5801

American Hanoverian Society
4059 Iron Works Pike,
Building C
Lexington, KY 40511
(606) 255-4141

American Holsteiner Horse
Association
222 East Main Street #1
Georgetown, KY 40324-1712
(502) 863-4239

American Horse Council
1700 K Street NW, Suite 300
Washington, DC 20006-3805
(202) 296-4031

American Horse Shows Association
220 East 42nd Street
New York, NY 10017-5876
(212) 972-2472

American Hunter and Jumper
Foundation
335 Lancaster Street
P.O. Box 369
West Boylston, MA 01583-0369
(508) 835-8813

American Miniature Horse
Association
2908 SE Loop 820
Fort Worth, TX 76140-1073
(817) 293-0041

American Morgan Horse Association
P.O. Box 960
Shelburne, VT 05482-0960
(802) 985-4944

American Mustang and Burro
Association
P.O. Box 788
Lincoln, CA 95648
(916) 633-9271

American Paint Horse Association
P.O. Box 961023
Fort Worth, TX 76161-0023
(817) 439-3400

American Quarter Horse Association
P.O. Box 200
Amarillo, TX 79168-0001
(806) 376-4811

American Riding Instructor
Certification Program
American Riding Instructors
Association
P.O. Box 282
Alton Bay, NH 03810-0282
(603) 875-4000

American Shetland Pony Club
6748 North Frostwood Parkway
Peoria, IL 61615
(309) 691-9661

American Trakehner Association
1520 West Church Street
Newark, OH 43055
(614) 344-1111

American Youth Horse Council
4093 Iron Works Pike
Lexington, KY 40511-2742
(800) 879-2942

Appaloosa Horse Club
P.O. Box 8403
Moscow, ID 83843-0903
(208) 882-5578

Appaloosa Sport Horse Association
1360 Saxonburg Boulevard
Glenshaw, PA 15116
(412) 767-4616

Arabian Horse Registry of America
12000 Zuni Street
Westminster, CO 80234-2300
(303) 450-4748

Arabian Sport Horse Association,
Inc.
6145 Whaleyville Boulevard
Suffolk, VA 23428
(804) 986-4486

Arizona Hunter Jumper Association
P.O. Box 13112
Scottsdale, AZ 85267
(602) 998-1596

Arizona State Horsemen's
Association
P.O. Box 31758
Phoenix, AZ 85046-1758
(602) 867-6814

Arkansas Horse Council
921 East Fifth Street
Texarkana, AR 75502-5419
(501) 774-8822

Bay State Trail Riders Association
24 Glenn Street
Douglas, MA 01516-2410
(508) 476-3960

Blue Ridge Hunter Jumper
Association
P.O. Box 752
Tryon, NC 28782
(803) 468-4688

California State Horsemen's
Association
325-B Pollasky Avenue
Clovis, CA 93612-1139
(209) 325-1055

Capital District Hunter Jumper
Council
3666 Carman Road
Schenectady, NY 12303
(518) 456-5010

Central Ohio Saddle Club
Association
11690 North Island Road
Grafton, OH 44044
(216) 748-2354

Central Pennsylvania Junior Horse
Show Association
RD #5 Chestnut Grove Road
Dillsburg, PA 17019
(717) 432-2688

Colorado Horsemen's Council
P.O. Box 1125
Arvada, CO 80001-1125
(303) 279-4546

Colorado Hunter and Jumper
Association
5415 South Federal Circle K102
Littleton, CO 80123-7738
(303) 347-2818

Combined Eastern Shore Horse
Shows
RD 6, Box 148
Millsboro, DE 19966
(302) 945-0734

Connecticut Horse Council
P.O. Box 905
Cheshire, CT 06410-0905
(860) 659-0848

Connecticut Hunter Jumper
Association
P.O. Box 571
South Windsor, CT 06074
(203) 648-9107

Deep South Hunter Jumper
  Association
3621 Kings Hill Road
Birmingham, AL 35223
(205) 967-9543

Delaware Equine Council
P.O. Box 534
Camden, DE 19934
(302) 398-5196

Friesian Horse Association of North
  America
2016 Grasmere Drive
Louisville, KY 40205
(512) 459-5676

Georgia Horse Council
P.O. Box 736
Dahlonega, GA 30533-0736
(706) 542-7023

Georgia Horse Foundation
525 Tullamore Way
Alpharetta, GA 30201
(404) 740-0983

Georgia Hunter-Jumper Association
400 Peach Drive
McDonough, GA 30253
(404) 914-1122

Gladstone Equestrian Association
Hamilton Farm
P.O. Box 119
Gladstone, NJ 07934-0119
(908) 234-0151

Greater Arkansas Hunter/Jumper
  Association
27 Stoneledge
Maumelle, AR 72113
(501) 851-1979

Greater Houston Horse Council
Route 4, Box 4372
Pearland, TX 77581
(713) 485-8154

Greater Houston Hunter/Jumper
  Association
7719 Clarewood
Houston, TX 77036
(713) 727-3669

Hawaii Horse Shows Association
2477 Halekoa Drive
Honolulu, HI 96821
(808) 538-4013

Horsemanship Safety Association
517 Bear Road
Lake Placid, FL 33852-9726
(941) 465-1365

Horsemen's Council of Illinois
6 North Walnut
Villa Grove, IL 61956
(217) 832-8419

Horse Shows and Exhibitors
  Association of Connecticut
70 Jackson Hill Road
Middlefield, CT 06455
(203) 347-9822

Hunter Jumper Association of
  Alabama
5424 Old Highway 280
Sterrett, AL 35147
(205) 678-9345

Hunter Jumper Exhibitors of
  Oklahoma
4030 South 132nd East Avenue
Tulsa, OK 74134
(918) 627-6206

Idaho Horse Council
5000 Chinden Boulevard
Boise, ID 83714
(208) 323-8148

Illinois Hunter and Jumper
    Association
1015 Harper Drive
Algonquin, IL 60102
(708) 658-7398

Indiana Horse Council
225 S. East Street, Suite 738
Indianapolis, IN 46202-4042
(317) 692-7115

Indiana Hunter and Jumper
    Association
2569 North Willow Way
Indianapolis, IN 46268
(317) 228-9343

Intercollegiate Horse Show
    Association
P.O. Box 741
Stony Brook, NY 11790-0741
(516) 751-2803

Inter-County Horsemen's
    Association
P.O. Box 111
Brookfield, OH 44403-0111
(216) 448-4683

International Side Saddle
    Organization
P.O. Box 73
Damascus, MD 20872
(301) 829-2116

Inter-State Horse Show Association
2607 Glenchester Road
Wexford, PA 15090
(412) 935-4751

International Buckskin Horse
    Association
P.O. Box 268
Shelby, IN 46377-0268
(219) 552-1013

Iowa Horse Industry Council
1817 East 30th
Des Moines, IA 50317
(515) 266-4734

Iowa Horse Shows Association
5255 Jenn Mill Road, SW
Riverside, IA 52327-9619
(319) 679-2794

Iowa-Nebraska Hunter/Jumper
    Association
7300 Northland Drive
Omaha, NE 68122-1908
(402) 571-0938

The Jockey Club
821 Corporate Drive
Lexington, KY 40503-2794
(800) 444-8521

Kansas Horse Council
1895 East 56 Road
Lecompton, KS 66050-4776
(913) 887-6422

Kentucky Horse Council
4089 Iron Works Pike
Lexington, KY 40511
(606) 255-5727

Kentucky Hunter/Jumper
    Association
271 Idle Hour Drive
Lexington, KY 40502
(606) 266-6937

Los Angeles Horse Shows
Association
480 Riverside Drive, Suite 1
Burbank, CA 91506
(818) 840-9337

Louisiana Hunter Jumper Association
P.O. Box 360
Covington, LA 70434
(504) 892-9712

Maine Equine Industry Association
4 Gabriel Drive, RR 4, Box 1254
Augusta, ME 04330-9441
(207) 622-4111

Maine Horse Association
P.O. Box 644
Springvale, ME 04083
(207) 490-2754

Marin Horse Council
171 Bel Marin Keys Boulevard
Novato, CA 94949-6183
(415) 883-4621

Maryland Horse Council
P.O. Box 4891
Timonium, MD 21093-4891
(410) 252-2100

Maryland Horse Shows Association
P.O. Box 497
Riderwood, MD 21139-0497
(410) 337-0681

Massachusetts Horsemen's Council
97 Walnut Street
East Douglas, MA 01516
(508) 476-3895

Michigan Horse Council
P.O. Box 22008
Lansing, MI 48909-2008
(517) 676-0122

Michigan Horse Show Association
6155 Hunters Creek
Imlay City, MI 48124
(810) 724-4817

Mid-American Horse Show
Association
1101 Peace Drive
Wheeling, IL 60090
(708) 537-4743

Minnesota Horse Council
13055 Riverdale Drive, NW
Box 202
Coon Rapids, MN 55448
(612) 922-8666

Minnesota Hunter and Jumper
Association
8131 140th Street North
Hugo, MN 55038
(612) 429-2037

Mississippi Horse Council
Route 1, Box 114
Tupelo, MS 38801-9721
(601) 842-9346

Mississippi Hunter Jumper
Association
P.O. Box 13904
Jackson, MS 39236-3904
(601) 354-0307

Missouri Equine Council
P.O. Box 692
Columbia, MO 65205-0692
(800) 313-3327

Missouri Horse Shows Association
2929 Concordia Lane
St. Charles, MO 63301
(314) 946-8727

Montana State Horse Shows
 Association
142 Third Street, South
Shelby, MT 59474-1940
(406) 434-5317

Naples Seahorse Riding Club
P.O. Box 10551
Naples, FL 33941
(813) 353-0058

Nassau Suffolk Horsemen's
 Association
2 Carll Court
Northport, NY 11768-1649
(516) 261-4915

National 4-H Council
7100 Connecticut Avenue
Chevy Chase, MD 20815-4999
(301) 961-2959

National Hunter and Jumper
 Association
P.O. Box 1015
Riverside, CT 06878-1015
(203) 869-1225

Nebraska Horse Council
P.O. Box 81481
Lincoln, NE 68501
(402) 434-8550

Nevada State Horsemen's
 Association
P.O. Box 10402
Reno, NV 89510
(702) 852-3011

New England Horsemen's Council
2032 East Main Road
Portsmouth, RI 02871-1226
(401) 683-1764

New Hampshire Horse Council
2 Old Governor's Road
Brookfield, NH 03872
(603) 522-6018

New Hampshire Horse and Trail
 Association
P.O. Box 160
Deerfield, NH 03037-0160
(603) 463-7924

New Jersey Horse Council
25 Beth Drive
Moorestown, NJ 08057-3021
(609) 231-0771

New Jersey Horse Shows
 Association
c/o Cynthia Porteous
3 Woodmont Road
Upper Montclair, NJ 07043-2535
(201) 783-4508

New Mexico Horse Council
P.O. Box 10206
Albuquerque, NM 87184-0206
(505) 344-8548

New Mexico Hunter/Jumper
 Association
P.O. Box 27406
Albuquerque, NM 87125
(505) 768-3397

New York State Horse Council
189 Strawtown Road
New City, NY 10956
(914) 639-9073

Norcal Hunter/Jumper Association
717 North McDowell Boulevard, #104
Petaluma, CA 94954
(707) 763-5554

North American Morab Horse
Association
W3174 Faro Springs Road
Hibert, WI 54129
(414) 853-3086

North American Riding for the
Handicapped Association
(NARHA)
P.O. Box 33150
Denver, CO 80233
(800) 369-RIDE
(303) 452-1212

North American Saddle Mule
Association
P.O. Box 1574
Boyd, TX 76023
(817) 433-BRAY

North American Trakehner
Association
P.O. Box 12172
Lexington, KY 40581
(502) 867-0375

North Carolina Horse Council
6921 Sunset Lake Road
Fuquay-Varina, NC 27526
(919) 552-3536

North Carolina Hunter and Jumper
Association
P.O. Box 1157
Matthews, NC 28106-1157
(704) 846-1035

Northeastern Pennsylvania
Horsemen's Association
P.O. Box 634
Waverly, PA 18471
(717) 378-2882

North Florida Hunter/Jumper
Association
P.O. Box 5116
Jacksonville, FL 32247-5116
(904) 641-4334

North Shore Horsemen's Association
P.O. Box 635
Byfield, MA 01922
(508) 462-3732

Northern Counties Hunter/Jumper
Association
P.O. Box 881
Orland, CA 95963
(916) 439-2145

Northwest Horse Council
1430 Willamette Street, #11
Eugene, OR 97401-4073
(503) 645-8928

Norwegian Fjord Association of
North America
24570 West Chardon Road
Grayslake, IL 60030
(708) 546-7881

Ohio Horsemen's Council
P.O. Box 316
Miamisburg, OH 45343-0316
(614) 653-0466

Oklahoma Hunter/Jumper
Association
6239 South Yorktown Place
Tulsa, OK 74136
(918) 743-8491

Orange County Horse Show
Association
P.O. Box 512
Trabuco Canyon, CA 92678
(714) 459-9611

Oregon Horse Council
P.O. Box 234
Cheshire, OR 97419-0234
(541) 998-2803

Oregon Horsemen's Association
2501 Westhills Road
Philomath, OR 97370
(541) 929-5493

Pacific Coast Horse Shows
Association
P.O. Box 5570
Glendale, CA 91221-5570
(818) 842-8194

Palm Beach County Horse Industry
Council
11409 Eagle's Nest Drive
Boynton Beach, FL 33437-4519
(407) 738-4773

Palomino Horse Association
HC63, Box 24
Dornsife, PA 17823
(717) 758-3067

Palomino Horse Breeders of America
15253 East Skelly Drive
Tulsa, OK 74116-2637
(918) 438-1234

Penn Ohio Horsemen's Association
6144 Mill Creek Boulevard
Boardman, OH 44512
(216) 758-8374

Pennsylvania Equine Council
P.O. Box 238
Noxen, PA 18636-0238
(717) 624-4263

Pennsylvania Horse Show
Association
8801 Cheltenham Avenue
Philadelphia, PA 19118-1125
(215) 822-2537

Pennsylvania Jumper Association
P.O. Box 454
Eagle, PA 19480-0454
(610) 458-7415

Percheron Horse Association of
America
P.O. Box 141
Fredericktown, OH 43019-0141
(614) 694-3602

Pinto Horse Association of America
1900 Samuels Avenue
Fort Worth, TX 76102-1141
(817) 336-7842

Pony of the Americas Club
5240 Elmwood Avenue
Indianapolis, IN 46203-5990
(317) 788-0107

Professional Horsemen's Association
of America
2009 Harris Road
Penfield, NY 14526
(716) 377-4986

Rhode Island Horsemen's
Association
1 Russett Road
Middletown, RI 02842
(401) 847-5459

Rocky Mountain Horse Shows
Association
13834 West 69th Avenue
Arvada, CO 80004-1107
(303) 421-1928

Sacramento Area Hunter/Jumper
Association
P.O. Box 2421
Granite Bay, CA 95746
(916) 791-2596

South Carolina Horsemen's Council
P.O. Box 11280
Columbia, SC 29211
(803) 734-2210

South Dakota Horse Council
45971 244 Street
Colton, SD 57018-5010
(605) 446-3613

South Florida Hunter and Jumper
Association
22397 SW 66 Avenue, #706
Boca Raton, FL 33428
(407) 487-6016

South Shore Horsemen's Council
58 Carriage Road
Hamson, MA 02341
(617) 826-4573

Southern Nevada Hunter/Jumper
Association
1611 Chesterfield
Henderson, NV 89014
(702) 454-0767

Southwest International
Hunter/Jumper Association
P.O. Box 35-3100
Canutillo, TX 79835
(505) 523-6046

Southwest Virginia Hunter/Jumper
Association
Route 1, Box 182-H
Glasgow, VA 24555-9767
(703) 258-1104

The Sunshine State Horse Council
P.O. Box 4158
North Fort Meyers, FL
33918-4158
(941) 731-2999

Swedish Warmblood Association of
North America
P.O. Box 1587
Coupeville, WA 98239-1587
(206) 678-3503

Tennessee Horse Council
P.O. Box 69
College Grove, TN 37046-0069
(615) 395-7650
(615) 297-3200

Texas Hunter and Jumper
Association
1632 Norfolk Street
Houston, TX 77006
(713) 529-9983

Thoroughbred Horses For Sport
P.O. Box 160
Great Falls, VA 22066
(703) 759-6273

Tri-County Riding Association
RD 3, Box 346
Valatie, NY 12184
(518) 392-9422

Tri-State Horse Shows Association
386 Canfield Drive
Ghanna, OH 43230
(614) 471-7811

Tri-State Horsemen's Association
50-91st Lane NE
Blaine, MN 55434
(612) 784-6593

United States Equestrian Team
Pottersville Road
Gladstone, NJ 07934
(908) 234-1251

United States Pony Clubs
4071 Iron Works Pike
Lexington, KY 40511-8462
(606) 254-PONY

Utah Horse Council
1170 West 1000 South
Logan, UT 84321
(801) 752-7701

Utah Hunter and Jumper Association
1458 Clayton Street
Salt Lake City, UT 84104
(801) 972-2667

Vermont Horse Council
P.O. Box 105
Montpelier, VT 05601
(802) 229-1006
(800) 722-1419

Vermont Horse Shows Association
RD 2, Box 166
South Royalton, VT 05068-9110
(802) 457-1792

Virginia Horse Council
2178 Mt. Tabor Road
Blacksburg, VA 24060-8910
(703) 552-0085

Virginia Horse Shows Association
32 Ashby Street, Suite 204
Warrenton, VA 22186-3346
(703) 349-0910

Washington State Horse Council
P.O. Box 40263
Bellevue, WA 98015-4263
(206) 451-1654

Washington State Horsemen
P.O. Box 1566
Yelm, WA 98597
(206) 458-6300

Washington State Hunter/Jumper
Association
10108 NE 68 #1
Kirkland, WA 98033
(206) 822-8195

Western Montana Horse Council
534 Ridge Road
Stevensville, MT 59870
(406) 777-3936

West Virginia Horsemen's
Association
Route 1, Box 250
Flemington, WV 26347
(304) 842-2220

Welsh Pony and Cob Society of
America
P.O. Box 2977
Winchester, VA 22604-2977
(540) 667-6195

Wild Horse of America Registry
6212 East Sweetwater Avenue
Scottsdale, AZ 85254-4461
(602) 991-0273

Wisconsin State Horse Council
    University of Wisconsin
1675 Observatory Drive
287 Animal Science Building
Madison, WI 53706-1284
(608) 263-4303

Wisconsin Hunter/Jumper
    Association
1463 Cedar Creek Parkway
Grafton, WI 53024
(414) 377-6068

World Sidesaddle Federation
P.O. Box 1104
Bucyrus, OH 44820
(419) 284-3176

MAJOR NORTH AMERICAN HORSE SHOWS

The following is a sampling of major shows to help you find horse shows in your region; it is not a definitive listing of every major horse show in the United States. AHSA members receive a complete guide annually, the Competition Calendar. Several magazines, including *Chronicle of the Horse,* print horse show dates and information on a monthly or quarterly basis. Contact the AHSA or your regional/state horse show association for more information.

January

Palm Springs Classic Horse Show and Desert Circuit Horse Shows in Indio, Calif.

Palm Beach Classic in Wellington, Fla.

February

Sundance Welcome in Tucson, Ariz.

Arizona Winter Festival in Goodyear, Ariz.

Indio Classic Horse Show and Desert Circuit Horse Shows in Indio, Calif.

Palm Beach Internationale, Tournament, Masters and Open in Wellington, Fla.

Mardi Gras Circuit in New Orleans, La.

March

American Invitational, Tournament of Champions, Tampa Bay Classic in Tampa, Fla.

April

Georgia Internationale Jumping Classic in Conyers, Ga.

Four Seasons Horse Shows in Allentown, N.J.

Maryland National in Culpeper, Va.

Spring Benefit Hunter Jumper Shows in Monroe, Wash.

May

Devon Horse Show in Devon, Pa.

Memorial Day Classic in Los Angeles, Calif.

Garden State Horse Show in Augusta, N.J.

Oaks Classic in San Juan Capistrano, Calif.

Hunter-Jumper Association of Michigan Horse Shows in Chelsea and Oxford, Mich.

Old Salem Farm Horse Show in North Salem, N.Y.

Pinehurst Horse Classic in Pinehurst, N.C.

Nashville Country Hunter and Jumper Show in Franklin, Tenn.

June

USET Festival of Champions in Gladstone, N.J.

Oxridge Charity Horse Show in Darien, Conn.

Fairfield County Hunt Club in Westport, Conn.

Roanoke Valley Horse Show in Roanoke, Va.

Motor City and Detroit Horse Shows in Bloomfield Hills, Mich.

Maplewood Jumping Festival in Reno, Nev.

World Wide Hunter Jumper Show in Albuquerque, N. Mex.

Lake Placid Horse Show in Lake Placid, N.Y.

Oklahoma Jumping Festival in Guthrie, Okla.

Blue Ribbon Hunter Jumper Shows in Irving and Glen Rose, Tex.

Upperville Colt and Horse Show in Upperville, Va.

July

Monterey National Hunter Jumper Show in Monterey, Calif.

I Love New York Horse Show in Lake Placid, N.Y.

New York Horse and Pony Show in Ellenville, N.Y.

Valley Classic and Sugarbush Horse Shows in Waitsfield, Vt.

Rocky Mountain Classic and Colorado Summer Classic Grand Prix in Parker, Colo.

August

Labor Day Classic in San Juan Capistrano, Calif.

Kentucky Hunter Jumper Association Horse Show and Blue Grass Festival in Lexington, Ky.

Stoneleigh Burnham Horse Show in Greenfield, Mass.

Attitash Equine Festival in Bartlett, N.H.

Hampton Classic in Bridgehampton, N.Y.

Newport Jumping Classic in Portsmouth, R.I.

AHSA/Millers Pony Finals in Gladstone, N.J.

Grandprix of Indianapolis in Zionsville, Ind.

September

Spruce Meadows Masters in Calgary, Alberta, Canada

Autumn Classic in Port Jervis, N.Y.

Los Angeles International Jumping Fest in Los Angeles, Calif.

Oaks Fall Classic in San Juan Capistrano, Calif.

Eastern States Exposition in West Springfield, Mass.

Midway Hunter Jumper Show in Columbia, Mo.

Buffalo International in Buffalo, N.Y.

American Gold Cup in Devon, Pa.

Culpeper Hunter Jumper Show in Culpeper, Va.

Kentucky National Show in Lexington, Ky.

October

Washington International Horse Show in Landover, Md.

Capital Challenge Hunter Jumper in Upper Marlboro, Md.

Pennsylvania National Horse Show in Harrisburg, Pa.

Quarter Horse Congress in Columbus, Ohio

Grand National and World Championship Morgan Horse Show in Oklahoma City, Okla.

November

Los Angeles National in Los Angeles, Calif.

National Horse Show in New York, N.Y.

Royal Agricultural Winter Fair in Toronto, Ontario, Canada

AQHA World Championship Show in Oklahoma City, Okla.

December

The Pines Open Horse Shows in South Glastonbury, Conn.

GLOSSARY

AHSA. American Horse Shows Association.

Azoturia. An abnormal condition that causes horses to walk stiffly, have very stiff and rigid muscles, sweat heavily, and sometimes have trouble passing urine. It's caused by an overabundance of lactic acid brought on by overwork, overfeeding grain, or poor management. Also called "tying up."

Barn manager. The person who oversees the operation of a stable including feeding, cleaning, and horse health concerns.

Breeches (pronounced *Britch-es*). Riding pants that are designed to be worn with tall field boots or dress boots.

Canter. A three-beat gait. The canter has either a left or a right lead. The order of leg movement is either off side rear, then the diagonal pair of off side foreleg with near side rear, and finally the near side foreleg; or near side rear, then the diagonal pair of near side foreleg with off side rear leg, and finally the off side foreleg.

Cantle. The rear portion of the saddle.

Chaps. Leather leggings that cover and protect your legs for riding. Chaps fasten around the waist, then cover the area from the hips to the ankles.

Coach. A person who instructs you in the art of showing, at shows and at home. Also called a trainer.

Coggins test. A blood test to detect the presence of equine infectious anemia (EIA or swamp fever). A horse must have a negative Coggins test result to compete at a horse show.

Colic. In simple terms, a bellyache. Colic is a serious illness in horses; it can be painful and difficult to treat.

Cooler. A type of blanket that's put on the horse after exercise or a bath to "cool" him down and help him dry.

Courses. A group of fences that are jumped in a specific order.

Cross-rails. Small fences used in beginner classes over fences. Two rails are crossed to create a low spot in the center of the jump, hence the name "cross-rails."

Diagonals. A diagonal refers to the post of the rider at the trot, depending on the direction of travel. When traveling in a clockwise fashion, the rider posts in time with the outside (in this case left) shoulder and should be on the left diagonal. This means the rider should be in the "up" portion of the post when the outside shoulder is forward, and sitting down when the outside shoulder swings back.

Division. A collection of related classes at a show.

Farrier. The person who shoes and trims a horse's hooves. Also called a blacksmith.

Faults. A penalty during the jumping performance. In jumper classes, common faults include refusals, knockdowns, and exceeding the time allowed. In hunter classes, common faults include poor movement and jumping form.

Frame. The manner in which the horse holds his body during exercise or show performance.

Gaits. The different movements and ways of moving forward on the flat. These include the walk, trot, canter, and hand gallop.

Good mover. A horse that has an even, long, ground-covering stride with very little excess knee action.

Grand Prix. The highest level in jumper classes, with large fences, tough competition, and high prize money.

Hand gallop. The same three-beat gait as the canter, but faster than a canter and slower than a gallop.

Heaves. A labored breathing condition caused by allergies, illness, or too much exercise.

Hunter classes. Classes in which the horse is judged on his jumping form, ability, overall appearance, manners, and movement under saddle ("way of going").

Hunter seat equitation classes. Classes in which the rider is judged on his horsemanship, position, and control of the horse.

Jodhpurs. Ankle-length pants for riding, generally worn with paddock or jodhpur boots.

Jumpers. A division in which the horse is judged on time and faults over fences only.

Laminitis. An inflammation of the sensitive laminae in the horse's hoof, causing severe lameness. Also referred to as "founder."

Leads. Horses have two leads at the canter, the left and the right. For example, when the horse's left front leg "leads," he's considered to be on the left lead. See "Canter."

Long stirrup division. A division for older or adult riders. It may include hunter and equitation classes.

Lunge line. A long rope that's attached to the halter or cavesson to lunge (exercise) the horse by having him move in circles around you. Lunge lines are made of cotton or nylon.

Movement. How the horse moves under saddle at the walk, trot, and canter.

Near side. The left side of the horse.

Off side. The right side of the horse.

On the flat. When equitation riders ride at the walk, trot, and canter.

Over fences. Any equitation or hunter class in which a course of fences is jumped.

Pleasure class. A class in which the horse is judged on his ability to give a good pleasure ride. The horse must move evenly, be mannerly, and act sensibly.

Pommel. The front portion of the saddle that's over the withers.

Pony. A small horse, measured at 14.2 hands and under. Ponies are separated into three different sizes for horse show purposes: small (under 12.2 hands), medium (over 12.2, up to 13.2 hands), and large (over 13.2, up to 14.2 hands).

Pony hunter classes. Hunter classes for ponies only.

Post entry fees. Entry fees for entering show classes after the closing date or on the day of the event, rather than in advance of the show.

Posting. The act of rising up and then sitting down in the saddle in rhythm with the horse's trot.

Prize list. The list of classes and divisions a horse show offers. Also called a *class* or *show list.*

Pulled mane. A mane that has been thinned and shortened with the aid of a mane or pulling comb.

Ratcatcher. A riding shirt with a high collar and choker.

Rating. A method of distinguishing shows by size and prize money offered. The AHSA rates shows in this manner.

Refusal. When a horse will not jump a designated fence.

Riding instructor. A person who teaches riding to students.

Schooling show. A show that's not rated by the AHSA and is run to give people experience.

Scope. Talent and ability.

Seat. The manner and form in which a rider sits on the horse.

Short stirrup division. A group of classes for young riders, usually under the age of thirteen.

Striding. The distance between fences on a course, measured in a horse's strides.

Tack. The equipment used on the horse to ride and control it. Examples are saddles, bridles, and halters. Tack can be made of leather or synthetic materials.

Tacking up. The act of putting the bridle and saddle on the horse in order to ride.

Trainer. A person who instructs you in the art of showing, at shows and at home. Also called a coach.

Trot. A two-beat gait in which the horse's legs work in diagonal pairs, left front with right rear and right front with left rear. You can post or sit to the trot.

Turnout vs. turning out. Turnout indicates the appearance and finish of a horse and rider. Turning out refers to the process of doing this, or to the act of setting loose a horse into a pasture.

Under saddle. A class in which a hunter performs at the walk, trot, and canter, and is judged on his movement and manners.

Veterinarian. A doctor for horses and other animals.

Walk. The slowest of the gaits, with four beats. The legs work in the order of near side rear, near side foreleg, off side rear, then off side foreleg.

Worms. Parasitic organisms that inhabit the intestinal tract of the horse.

Index